"Corletta Vaughn's "*Teach Your Daughters to Fly*" is a welcome and much needed book for today's dads. It will help many men, at anytime of fatherhood, see how they can emotionally mentor their daughters. It will inspire them to see the potential they can unlock in their daughters, and by helping their girls they will uncover something of profound value for themselves as men. Nothing can change a man like becoming a father, and when you have a daughter this is the book you want to read!"

Bruce Linton, Ph.D.
Founder of the Fathers' Forum
Author of "*Becoming a Dad, how fatherhood changes men*"
www.fathersforum.com

"Dr. Corletta Vaughn cuts straight to the core with her passionate and accurate teachings, and says, 'NO MORE LAME EXCUSES, DAD!' Fathers are in for a wakeup call that will help change not only their lives, but the lives of their daughters."

Todd McBroom
Author of *God Was Self Employed*
www.ToddMcBroom.com

"As a Father myself, I am thankful that Dr. Corletta Vaughn has written 'Teach Your Daughters to Fly.' This book drives a crucial message to fathers everywhere to embrace their children and encourage them to follow their dreams."

Chris Swanson
Author of *Tinman to Ironman*
www.SwansonLeadership.com

3

"Bishop Corletta Vaughn is truly inspiring and her message is one that will help fathers raise daughters of Christ for generations to come."

Candace Mann

Author of the *Parker Valley Series*

www.ParkerValleySeries.com

"In *'Teach Your Daughters to Fly'* Dr. Corletta Vaughn truly captures the importance of the father-daughter relationship. She speaks to fathers in a strong but understanding tone, and teaches them the reasons behind their confusion concerning their daughters, while providing tangible tools to build an unbreakable bond."

Talayah Stovall,

Author of *Light Bulb Moments: 75 Lessons for Everyday Living* and *Crossing the Threshold: Opening Your Door to Successful Relationships*

www.TalayahStovall.com

"Fatherhood is a never ending process, no matter the age, difference, or circumstances. To be a father once, is to be a father for always. Being a father is leading your child into greatness, and helping them to grow and learn. Dr. Vaughn brings to light the answers to many questions that father's have, making it known that even when we feel we are failing, there is always a way to make things better, and to strengthen the relationships we have with our daughters."

Clifton Cottom

Author of *Asia's New Wings*

www.AsiaCottom.com

TEACH YOUR DAUGHTERS TO FLY

TEACH YOUR DAUGHTERS TO FLY

CORLETTA J. VAUGHN

NEXT CENTURY
PUBLISHING

Teach Your Daughters to Fly

Published by Next Century Publishing
Las Vegas, NV
www.NextCenturyPublishing.com

ISBN: 978-1-62903-830-8

Library of Congress Control Number: 2015935941

Printed in the United States of America

This book is dedicated to my beloved Daddy,
Mentor and Flight Instructor
Henry Nathaniel Lewis
1902-1993

To My 2 Beautiful Children
Shannon Marie
Apprille Nichole

Your arrivals gave me the BEST TWO days of my
life. Girls, Keep Flying, Keep Soaring!

TEACH YOUR DAUGHTERS TO FLY

Table of Contents

Introduction

In the movie *Fly Away Home*, a young girl, whose Mother has died in a car accident, must now live with her long estranged Father. He brings her to his home in Canada, where she must grieve her loss and adjust to living with a Father she barely knows. The film uses the beauty of nature and an orphaned gaggle of goslings to illustrate the process through which the daughter heals. The movie also describes how the Father learns to be a good parent.

I first watched this movie in 1996. It captured me! In fact, the plot, the characters, and the outcome kept my attention for days on end. While I loved the fact that the geese were saved, what really caught my attention was the transformation that happened in Amy Alden's life. We watched her change from a hurt-filled thirteen-year-old who wanted nothing to do with her Dad to a confident young lady whose self-confidence and self-image began to take flight, and who, in the process, learned some valuable life lessons.

But Amy would never have completed her mission had it not been for her Father. Thomas Alden saw more than his daughter; he saw a leader. She was someone capable of greatness. And he was willing to do whatever she needed.

While I was growing up, Henry N. Lewis, my Dad, was a phenomenal Dad. Everything that I've achieved and continue to be successful in is because of the early life lessons my Father taught me. He gave me my confidence; he gave me my perspectives; he gave me my worldview; and he helped me define my life beyond my gender. He never treated me like a "girl" who was limited to only what the "world" gave to females. He always made me believe that I could do *anything*. He would teach me the necessary strategies and skillsets for my life's journey. Because of his investing in me on this level, I learned ingenuity in business, finance, relationships, and the foundation of my relationship with God.

I believe every Father can do the same thing that my Dad did, and I endeavor to show you in this book the different methodologies needed to make you a phenomenal Dad. The greatest thing a Father can do for his daughter is to believe in her, and let nothing separate him from speaking into her life at important moments that will define who she is for the rest of her life.

Even though I was a typical girl, he saw someone atypical. When I questioned too much and others tried to hush me, he saw a thirst for knowledge. When I was rebellious, he saw someone willing to go against the status quo. And when I began to mature, he saw leadership, self-confidence, and much more!

I wrote this book not just to tell you about Amy or even me—although I parallel our stories to give you examples and illustrations. I wrote it to help *you*, Dad, see that your daughter has greatness in her. Dad, it is up to you to see who your daughter was created to be, to see her gifts and talents, and to do everything you can to bring her into her destiny.

Now, I understand that might seem intimidating to you. She is a female and you are a male, and that alone can be enough to make you run in the other direction! But in the pages you are about to read, you will find the ways and means to begin to engage your daughter on a different level—a "destiny" level. I will show you things about your daughter that you may never have realized were there. I will give you practical examples and ways to help her live her life in such a way that she naturally steps into what she was created for, and to help you give her the "flight plans" needed to help her soar.

I am in your corner, Dad. I am with you every step of the way. So read what I have written. Take it to heart. Ponder it. Ask God to show you who your daughter is. And by the time you have finished reading this book, you will know how to *teach your daughter to fly!*

I believe in you! And I believe your daughter can fly!

Corletta J Vaughn

"Every Girl is Someone's Daughter"
–Olivia Pope

CHAPTER 1

●●●

"It's a Girl!"

The moment you realize that your newborn is not a boy but a girl is the moment you must reevaluate your parenting contribution.   Dad, if you were expecting a son, you now have to think about all that you had planned for your new son, and to now begin a new development strategy to raise your daughter.

To be actively involved and charter a winning course for her for the rest of her life, you are sometimes going to be lost and befuddled if you don't design a game plan for this girl right now.   Please, don't be disappointed that you did not have a son!

You have been given a precious gift that can reproduce all that you have and then some. With the right guidance and support this little bundle of joy you will wrap in a pink blanket instead of blue will bring all your dreams to pass and do it with great admiration and respect for her initial caregivers.

After reading the introduction you know that one of my all-time favorite movies is called "Fly Away Home". It was while I was watching this movie years ago that I was reminded how important the father-daughter relationship is and that's when the idea for this book first came into my mind.

In the course of life, I have run into tremendous women—wives, daughters, Moms, in every stream of life and livelihood—from continents far away and villages unknown, to the country and slow towns of America; women of different colors, perspectives, languages, races, and religions. Within these women, I've found a common thread of strength that is a much deeper connection than what appears on their faces and in their well-groomed appearances. There's a confidence in their own worth and purpose that is defined by the Fathers in their lives. Sadly, and just as often, I've met women with a weakness or dimness in the eyes that can be traced back to their lack of a Father, this prominent person in a woman's early years—to his absence, mistreatment, or abandonment of her.

What makes one woman balanced, vital, passionate, and purposed, while another woman is small, silent, shriveled, and pained; or aggressive, angry, and afraid? The difference between these two women is what I call "Father-Hunger," a term I have coined through the years of teaching, counseling and pastoring. Father-Hunger implies the absence of a Father, but it is so much more than that. It is the absence of constraints, protection, and boundaries, as well as the absence of worth, values and fearlessness. When the Father of a girl is not emotionally and physically present, it doesn't matter what he can provide for her—she will always have a hunger in the deepest parts of her soul for him. She needs to feel him value her *every* day in *every* way. Physically, audibly, spiritually, and emotionally, she needs her Father every day to push, define, dare, and provoke her to be a giant, to get up from a fall, to rebound beautifully from disappointment, to take wings and fly.

A Father is a daughter's first image of a man as a Dad, date, provider, protector, and the role model of a husband. Without a Dad in her life, a young lioness will have to hunt for her own food, find self-esteem and look for protective boundaries from others. It has been providentially ordained that she should be always "covered" by this first male in her life. He should never expose her nakedness and vulnerability, but revere and respect her. A dad is so important to a girl's life; statistics prove that when a girl is Fatherless, she is prone to violence, promiscuity, vanity, and disease, among many other downfalls in life. His absence impacts her mentally, socially, spiritually, and physically. Her appearance, style, confidence, and assertiveness are determined by her Dad. It is this man who will shape her for success or for painful failure from the very first days of her life.

My Dad was so tremendous in my life, and I know that most of the credit for whatever I have already achieved and have become good at is because of this one primary attribute: My Father was always in the home, in my life, and at the dinner table. His words and model forever remain indelible on my character and conscience. My precious Mother, Jessie A. Lewis, had a supportive, loving husband, and she taught me the beauty of being covered, adored, and respected through the way she responded to my Dad's love for her.

Girls NEED their Dads to love their Mothers and help create an atmosphere of safety and provision for all of their children; the entire family has a great advantage when Father-Hunger is NOT an issue.

Father-Hunger is huge; in my opinion, it is the No. 1 issue in a girl's life. Yet it is rampant in the world today, and this hunger creates what I call a "spirit of the orphan." People who are influenced by this "spirit" cannot connect with others. They have trouble with social systems; they have trouble with relationships; they have trouble with intimacy; and they have serious trouble with commitment.

Why do your daughters need to hear your voice as their Father? You provide order. You set the laws. You provide boundaries. That's why your daughters need to hear *your* voice.

The Father, the man, innately wants to set boundaries for his family. He has a design for his family. He has a template—what his family is to be or look like—and from his template, a Father defines his absolutes. His absolutes are about the other people in his life and how he foresees their development. For instance, when I was becoming of dating age, around fifteen or sixteen, my Daddy told me, "If you are not home by the time the street lights are on, don't bother trying to come in the house." As I grew older, the curfew changed to 1 a.m., but it was still an absolute. Daddy said, "If you aren't in the house by 1 a.m., then you can sleep on the porch." I am sixty-one-years-old now, and I can still hear his voice and I still obey what he told me. What he said was for *my* protection, and I'm still home by 1 a.m. today. It is an absolute.

One of the Father's responsibilities is to set the guidelines for the family. There are times for discussion and times for boundary setting. What is absolute with a Father should be left as is. Mothers may negotiate, but what a Father has resolved in his mind should be what it is, as long as it benefits all involved. Yes, this is hard at times for everyone; but what a Father has decided in his mind is for the well-being of his daughter. Sometimes Daddy has to say, "You eat when we eat, you eat what your Mama cooks, and you wear what we bought you." As a Dad, you have to say no a lot. You have to stand your ground with your daughter. And she'll be upset, and she'll upset you. But a Father's absolutes will protect his daughter.

Today many women are fragile. They're fragile because they don't know the voice of their Father. They don't know the boundaries set by a caring, protective Father, and they don't know the authority of a good Father. They don't know what a Father does. This lack of knowing a real Dad creates lifestyle patterns, unwholesome ones, with lifelong effects that are tragic. Lives are squandered when daughters don't have Dads actively involved in their development. Because they don't know the voice of their Father, they break easily and get offended easily, and they lash out when they do hear the sound of authority or feel the pressure of authority.

The Father provides guidelines. He gives the definition of who his daughter is. He is there to monitor her and to help interpret life for her.

The Father is the gatekeeper, the safety patrol. He has to be careful to watch the people who come around his daughter. The Father interprets truths and facts the daughter cannot see: "That boy is not for you." "That girl is not your friend." "You can go to that friend's house but you can't go to that other person's house." He has clear boundaries of yes and no.

A Father is the daughter's first protector, because Fathers make their daughters feel safe. That is why so many women don't know that they should feel safe; they never had their Father's protection from the time they were newborns onward.

I was always safe. Even when something, or someone, tried to violate me, my Father eliminated the threat; most times, I never knew it was there and never even knew when the threat left. I never had to worry about whether or not someone was going to attack me, because my Father was always present, always watchful.

That's what a Father does. My Father protected me. Protected me from boys, from dogs, from systems, and from other sources of hatred and hurt; my Father was my first line of defense against anything that would make me feel unsafe.

Fathers should always model good behavior because they leave a lasting imprint. My Father imprinted me as a child and throughout his life, into my adulthood. Mr. Lewis was a careful steward of his family, and he taught me through direct and indirect lessons, modeling, and teaching, sometimes verbally and sometimes nonverbally.

When a daughter comes into the world, she is pure and undefiled. And a Father's first responsibility toward her is to maintain her innocence and to make sure that she is protected. So, as a Father, you have to keep her pure and position her for success in the world. My Father did exactly that; he worked to keep me pure from vices, habits, relationships, or any encounters that would compromise my innocence.

Fathers protect. They also challenge infrastructures to help their daughters understand what is and isn't good for them. If infrastructures need to be challenged, Fathers should do that for their daughters.

My Father gave me a legacy. You can give a legacy to your daughters and not just to your sons. If your daughter is going to fly, she needs wings, and the legacy you give her will be the wings that she needs to lift off and fly. Wings, on airplanes and birds, are shaped to produce aerodynamic force. On most airplanes, wings are usually relatively flat on the bottom, rounded at the front, and convex across the top, tapering at the trailing edge. The shape forces air to move faster over the top, which lowers the air pressure on top of the wing, causing the wing to rise. In the same way that wings provide lift for the airplane, a man's legacy provides lift for his daughter.

It is a proven fact that girls who have healthy, ongoing relationships with their Fathers during adolescence have less psychological stress in adult life than girls whose Fathers were absent. Franklin B. Krohn and Zoe Bogan of the State University of New York at Fredonia, in their 2001 paper on the effects of Father absence that appeared in the *College Student Journal,* noted:

> *Females whose Fathers died before the age of five are extremely reticent among male adults. They shy away from physical contact with them and rarely smile ... while daughters of divorce tend to be clumsily erotic. Daughters of divorce seek much more attention from men and have more physical contact with boys their age than girls from intact homes. They tend to be more critical of their Fathers and the opposite sex. ... These females constantly seek refuge for their missing Father. And as a result, there's a constant need to be accepted by men, from whom they aggressively seek attention. ... Girls who have [limited or disrupted] contact with their Fathers, especially in adolescence, had great difficulty forming lasting relationships with men. Sadly, these women either withdraw from men altogether or become sexually aggressive.*[1]

So then, women who have no Fathering become desperate for male attention. This is Father-Hunger and a need for affirmation. I have seen this hunger and this need in many women who are having emotional attachment issues or are having issues with their physical health, and such infirmities are consistent and unrelenting. I can sit down with a grown, adult woman who is fifty-five years past her childhood, talk with her for five minutes, and tell if she has Father-Hunger.

I know a young woman who struggled for years with migraine headaches. She lived with her Mom and Stepdad.

After talking to this woman, I suggested that she visit her real Father, with whom she had a good relationship. A few weeks later, she came to me and said, "I cannot believe how good I feel. My Dad and I started talking and I got up the courage to ask him questions I've always wanted to ask: Why did you leave? Why didn't you visit me? I haven't had a migraine for weeks now, whereas I used to get them about once a week." I see this type of scenario over and over, manifesting in fibromyalgia, arthritis, even breast and cervical cancer. I've known women who have been barren, but for no physical reason; they have instead been consumed with Father-Hunger.

Since the way a woman responds emotionally to a man is so consistent, it is easy to see if she is being vulnerable, or if she is strong. Is she contributing in the relationship or is she just receiving and accepting? When I am counseling a woman, I open up our session in terms of Father-Hunger: "Let's talk about your Father; I think that may be your struggle." Ten times out of ten, the woman starts crying, because no one has ever before touched her place of hurt. We treat symptoms, and the woman with Father-Hunger issues has treated it by trying to have relationship after relationship with men, or with spirituality, or with drugs, food, or entertainment, all in an effort to medicate her Father-Hunger.

Without a nurturing Father figure, a woman of any age doesn't know the voice of authority, the voice of a protector, or the sound of a boundary being placed. Today, women who don't know the voice of their Father become wounded by the voice of correction instead of understanding that someone is trying to instill structure or accountability. Instead, any and all male voices hurt these women, because they have never known the voice of a true Father.

How many girls get married before they're ready because they want "a man" in their lives? How many women take up with a man and get pregnant, and then abandon the relationship, simply because they want "that man" they've lacked? Father-Hunger is rampant, and it leads to perversions. Father-Hunger opens the door to lesbianism, and it leads many men into homosexuality.

How do we stem the tide? You stem it by being a phenomenal Father.

Your daughter needs to see life through your eyes. She needs to see through her Father's eyes because that's going to take her through the rest of her life. When she sees the world through the lenses of her Father's eyes, she feels safe. If she goes where she doesn't have her Father's permission to go, then she's going to get hurt. So your daughter should understand life through your eyes.

If she is going to fly, a girl's Father will become her air traffic controller, directing her takeoffs and landings. I don't mean "get off the ground." I don't mean "glide" or putter around in a little flying contraption. I mean teaching her to soar like an eagle. Did you know that eagles are strong enough to fly OVER storms? In fact, they fly FASTER over storms, and HIGHER. They can see farther and get there quicker. Give your daughter eagles' wings.

As a male, you have a God-given responsibility toward your daughters. What are you doing? You may be providing shelter, clothing, food, health care, and education. But are you modeling? Are you imprinting? Are you reaching in, talking, and engaging with your daughters? Are you nurturing your daughters by setting boundaries, instilling discipline, reproof, and teaching? And are you prepared to give permission to her as she grows, so that she can move forward without being codependent?

Giving her a blanket of security is your responsibility. It is your first obligation. She may become uncomfortable under that blanket sometimes. She will want out from under the blanket many times. And many times you'll have to stand on your absolutes, because you know she's not ready yet. Sometimes, you must give her permission to spread her wings a little, to discover her own strength, to see what flying solo is all about. That is a scary time for Dad.

Men have a difficult time with their emotions, and a daughter will prick those emotions; she's going to touch every one of them. She'll make her Daddy cry. Your daughter may close off as she becomes a teenager; she may blow up and find boys. It's an issue for every Dad and daughter when boys come around.

If she's getting the nurturing love from her Dad that she deserves, she'll make healthy choices in her love life. But even with all your imprinting, you will still have to keep watch on her. Being a Father doesn't end at age eighteen or when your little girl marries. You still must watch and protect.

Nurture your daughter. Teach her how to respond to a man as a healthy woman. Respect the God-given formula: The man initiates, the woman responds. If you respect her, and teach her, and protect her, your daughter's going to respond better to the males in her life when you're not around. One way or the other, she's going to respond to a man, because that's in her, to respond. So Dad, teach your daughter the proper response.

Dad also needs to know when it is right to give his daughter permission. At certain junctures, it's your role as a Father to give your daughter permission. This begins to occur very early in a girl's life and continues at each juncture when a daughter has learned the lessons of responsibility and accountability from her Father. It's a series of permissions, and there will be many, such as permission to answer the phone and talk to a boy, or permission to go on a date, or permission to stay out past curfew on prom night, or permission to use the car. The right time for each girl varies, and the permissions become more significant as she grows into adulthood. Dad needs to know when it is right to give permissions and when it is too soon or too early.

Fathers, teach your daughters to fly! It's important that daughters be made ready before adulthood. Your daughters' overall well-being—emotional, physical, mental and financial—will help to heal other people.

Every human is born of a woman; no man who is born is born of a man. Your daughter has the potential to birth children into the world, and your responsibility as Father is to nurture your daughter from birth so that when she becomes a Mother, she can train her children. They may be future presidents, CEOs, principals, doctors, lawyers, judges, ministers, inventors, and entertainers who will impact culture as we now know it. This is a responsibility worthy of who she is—and you are where this starts! Dad, own the fact that out of your body came seed that produced this child, and that what you provide as her Father sets her boundaries, morals and character traits. These will inevitably be transferred to her children and train them for their future productivity.

Father-Hunger doesn't go away until a Father comes back to his rightful place as mentor, and it's never too late. What are you going to do about your seed? Set her up for success, because that is what great Dads do; and if you believe in your daughter, you will make everybody else believe in her, too.

TAKEAWAYS

- How can you become your daughter's first protector and make her feel safe?
- How are you nurturing your daughter and what are you teaching her about male-female relationships?
- Do you recognize any Father-Hunger in your daughter? What can do you to alleviate it?

CHAPTER 2

●●●

When Dad is Missing-in-Action

"Dad?" says Amy... "Is that you?"

At the start of *Fly Away Home*, Thomas Alden was not a part of his daughter's life by choice and default. There was a divorce between him and Amy's Mom, and he did not continue with regular visits or the nurturing of his daughter. After the accident that claimed the Mother's life, he came into Amy's life in a hospital room when she was around thirteen-years-old. She was injured, bruised and bandaged from the car crash that had killed her Mother. When she awakened after the accident, she looked up at this man in the room and asked a question: "Dad?" She wasn't sure who he was. She didn't know him. In this pivotal moment of the film, you realize that this Father had walked away from his duty as family leader, and his daughter is now questioning his identity.

What is the impact on the child who doesn't have the Father in the home? What is the impact on a daughter's life when the identity of her Dad is unknown and his appearance is missing from her daily course of life?

"Father-child interactions have been shown to promote a child's physical well-being, perceptual abilities, and competency in relating to others."[2] "A survey of over 20,000 parents found that when Fathers are involved in their children's education, including attending school meetings and volunteering, children are more likely to get A's."[3] Fathers who are not invested in the relationship with the Mother of the child are less likely to be invested in the nurturing of their children, and tend to be more ambivalent about their responsibility to them. This is an atrocity seen throughout America, where the relationship with the Mother is compromised through many differing factors, so the child suffers for lack of the paternal care and involvement that he or she needs.

One of the most significant days of a girl's life is the day she gets married. And the tradition is that her Father should walk her down the aisle and then give her away to the husband she is about to be married to. Is this picture of marriage relevant today, in which the Father is the last person to have responsibility for her until she meets her husband?

Not too many days ago, I was a guest at a wedding in which the bride entered the church coming down the aisle alone. Both Father and Mother were alive and present in the services; at the time when the vows called for, "Who gives this woman away?," the question was omitted. This is a travesty of order and because there had been a lack of a

Father's presence in the young woman's life, he was only allowed to *attend* the wedding. He was not permitted in these final moments of her singlehood to *participate*. So the new husband received his new bride from no one. What will be the impact of her Father-Hunger in their marriage?

To me, this imagery represented a very defiant, angry and pained young woman, angry with her Father, defiant to her husband and pained in the deepest part of her heart for what she has never known, because there has been no Father's voice in her life. She has been her own voice. She has been her own guide. She has set her own boundaries; therefore, all the rules of her life are hers. How will this woman now respond to her new husband's voice and leadership in the traditional sense of marriage?

Remember that everything in creation is male and female, giver-receiver. Plants, electricity, even tools: Everything's male and female. One gives, one receives. The female is a responder. The male is the giver, the provider, and the protector. When did Fathering fall away? Is this not a travesty? Is this not a safe structure now compromised by missing-in-action Dads? Why do Fathers appear to be in touch with their created purpose in the plant and animal kingdoms, while in the human kingdom, which is the most superior, there is so much confusion and abdication of responsibility by Dads?

Throughout history, men have failed to protect, nurture and advocate for women, for their own wives, for women in general, and for daughters in particular. Men have sneaked away from the role of provider. They have walked away from their duties of Father and family leader.

Not only have they switched roles, from providers to receivers, but men have also lost their respect for the value of their own offspring. Women have become property, not helpmates. Even today, men still perceive their daughters to be of less value than their sons. Worse, men have failed to protect their daughters. Most perverse of all is the fact that some men have even become their daughters' predators.

Simply put, in defining this "travesty of order," the traditional design and respective roles of males and females have changed. Economics and job availability have made it possible for both parents to be in the workforce, so both parents are now removed from the home. It negates some of the Fathering needed in the home can be missing and replaced by money. Remember, money will never replace time spent with your child. Where there are resources, sometimes a live-in nanny or caregiver is providing the primary care of the child, and although this might be a valuable asset, Dad, it will never replace your time with your daughter.

Quality time spent by the Father with his daughter should take precedence even with Dad working. Beware of being "over-employed." He should be in the home with the daughter, but today, he is home less and less frequently; this is a sociological problem in which men have made women responsible for their children. When the Dad is not present, this puts tremendous, and unnatural, pressure on the Mother to provide the support that requires two parents.

Divorce is a major contribution to the travesty, in that most men do not get full custody of the children. Their only responsibility is child support, with some "visitation." But isn't child support more than a check? Child support should include active parenting, nurturing by presence, building bonds by spending time, and imprinting. Doesn't being a parent take more than two weekends out of a month plus maybe a summer? Can a child really be positively nurtured on these terms?

Another thing that can create travesty of order is educational achievement. Statistics prove that there are far more female college graduates than males—beginning in the 1970s and continuing today[4]—and, therefore, men have become more and more invisible in viable jobs in the marketplace due to their lack of education. This impacts men's self-esteem and self-worth is a very big way. Without the educational success of their female counterparts, they can feel less than adequate to speak into their daughters' lives because they don't have the education, and they give the wife or Mother more responsibility.

Children are born out of wedlock more often than we realize. In 2012, two out of every five newborns, 40.7 percent of all births in America, were born to unmarried parents—an increase from 33 percent a decade earlier.[5] This startling statistic is an obvious reason for disorder in the home and certainly creates chaos and silent suffering. This, too, is a travesty of the original order of marriage, which is for marriage to *precede* childbirth. The effect of this travesty can be brutal on both the child and the society.

Without the security of marriage, the Dad has no emotional commitment to parenting the child, which will most likely lead to the Mother supporting the family and being primarily responsible for raising the child. Without the commitment of marriage, a man may abdicate his responsibility, and since he is not married, no one can hold him to the responsibility of being present every day in his child's life. The number of children living with never-married Mothers grew from 221,000 in 1960 to 5.862 million in 1995.[6] The number of live births to unmarried women went from 224,300 in 1960, to 1.248 million in 1995,[7] to 1.42 million in 2003, to 1.607 million in 2012.[8]

While Fathers as single custodial parents are more common than in the past, they still account for less than 17 percent of all custodial single parents. Women head most single-parent homes.[9]

When only one parent raises the daughter, the girl is limited in her understanding of relationships, and that can hinder her view of life and social connectivity, as well as dating and marriage. She can suffer emotional pain and never understand why she is hurting. Father-Hunger is a real challenge to the mental and emotional health of a daughter and can have severe effects on her total well-being. Feelings of rejection and abandonment are paramount and can lead to low self-esteem issues, as well as to a daughter's inappropriate views about sexuality and relationships.

With so many missing-in-action Dads, the subject of men's mental health needs our close examination. Because poor mental health in men does not always look like what it does in women, it can be hard to recognize.

For example, a man who appears to have anger issues may actually be depressed. Aggression, argumentativeness, isolation, drug and alcohol use, loss of interest in hobbies, work and relationships are all signals that Dad is not well.

"Underemployment," lack of focus, lack of footing, lack of interest, restlessness, and fatigue are symptoms of depression's onset. Also, most men do not openly discuss their emotions like women do. That lack of openness impairs their ability to get the help they really need to confront the depressive symptoms and mood swings, since men often equate their manhood with the need to appear invincible.

Depression can take a man out of the picture of his family's life, and while he looks OK, he is really isn't. Feelings of anxiety, depletion, stress, and worry are toxic to any relationship and will make a man unavailable to intimate and meaningful socialization until the stressor is identified and removed.

Men, seek professional help if any of these feelings are now present in your life, not just for your daughter's sake, but for yours as well. You are important and must take care of your emotional and mental health on a consistent basis as a matter of priority. Remember that mental health issues are treatable and common. Don't feel stigmatized if you have needed to talk with a counselor. Get help early, so that you don't open doors to other complicating factors, such as medicating yourself with drugs, sexual perversion, pornography, or other delusional behavior. Get help and treatment early; at the first sign of being slightly overwhelmed, make the call.

Your physical health is VERY important and must be a priority in your mind if you are to carry out your assignment as a Father for the long term. Take a look at your weight, diet, prostate, exercise, heart, and overall health. Men, you have to be alive to be present and active in your daughter's life. Your physical wellness is your most valuable asset; so don't play around with this. If you are not healthy, you will not have the strength to participate in the vigor of parenting.

Being an active Dad in your daughter's life requires your action and activity on a consistent basis. If you don't feel well, or you feel sluggish, or your diet is out of whack, you will not want to take the extra steps of involvement. Get your check-ups regularly and be alive for a long time to come. Don't let sickness or a death take you out of action. The early death of a girl's father is traumatic for the entire family and can create damaging effects of loss and fear for the remainder of the girl's life, so take good care of yourself.

Be around a long time for your daughter and be a healthy, supportive man for her all of your life, as you were intended to be. This is so very important for her flight takeoffs and landings.

Your presence really does matter!

TAKEAWAYS

- Take an honest look at your relationship with your daughter. What is it *really* like?
- What "destiny" do you see in your daughter?
- How can you begin to come alongside her to help her become the person she was created to be?

CHAPTER 3

●●●

"That's a really lame excuse, dad"

"So where were you? Why didn't you come and see me?"

When a Father has been absent from a daughter's life and reappears, as in the movie *Fly Away Home*, there must be a confrontation and a day of reckoning with accountability. If you have watched the movie, you will recall a very private moment between the daughter, Amy Alden, and her Father, in which she asks him, "Why did you rarely come to see me when I lived with Mom?"

"Well, New Zealand's pretty far away," Dad replies.

Her response is simple and profound: "That's a really lame excuse, Dad."

Through the years, her response has stuck with me. I have heard so many Dads give empty reasons why they're not in their daughters' lives. I've also watched a daughter's eyes fill with tears as he speaks about his absence so nonchalantly, with no understanding of the pain he has caused. It's simply lame. I wonder how many men continue to make lame excuses for being an absent Father.

Here are some of the excuses I've heard:

- "I have to provide for my family."
- "I don't really know what my daughter needs."
- "Her Mom does a better job."
- "I know what to do with a boy. No one taught me what to do with a girl."
- "I'm afraid."
- "I make sure she has everything she needs."
- "Her Mother and I don't get along."
- "If I say something, her Mother's going to change it anyway, so what's the point?"
- "She's growing up so fast."
- "I'm busy."
- "I don't have any money."
- "When I get home, I'm really tired."

Do any of these excuses resonate with you? Are any of them justifiable reasons for your abdication of responsibility?

Let's look at the word "abdication" for a minute. "Abdication" can be both a noun and a verb. It means: 1. An act of abdicating or renouncing the throne. 2. Failure to fulfill a responsibility or duty, disowning, renunciation, rejection, refusal, relinquishment, repudiation. Synonyms: ABANDONMENT, "an abdication of responsibility."

The reasons men give to justify in their own minds their abdication of their Fatherly duties can go on forever. *But the truth is that every Father has an obligation toward his daughters as long as he and they are alive.* Regardless of the circumstances between parents, you, Dad, must make your daughter a priority.

Does anger toward your daughter's Mother keep you from knowing your daughter? Divorces, relationship breakups, an inability to relate to your daughter's Mother— these are simply excuses for letting your daughter grow up without her Father. Your daughter needs you now! No matter how long you've been out of her life, she needs you to resume your role as Father, protector, and provider; and she needs to hear your voice again in her ear.

Mom and Dad conflicts make it easy to fail and not follow through with the father obligation, but difficulties with daughter's Mother are not reasons for a Father's absence or abdication of parental responsibility. Sometimes the drama is not with the Mother of the child, but with the man's own Father-Hunger, which can cause him to disclaim Fatherhood.

Selfishness is really behind all of it. When a man doesn't take responsibility for his seed, it is because that's what he wanted to do; that's what he *chose* to do. His wants were higher than her needs. A man will do what he really wants to do, and then turn around and make an excuse for what he did not really want to do. And it all equals selfishness. In the ear of your daughter, your reasons and excuses sound like empty words. What you are really saying to her is that she is not a priority in your life, that she is not important enough for you to change your schedule to meet her need for your presence. You're telling her that:

- Your work and hobbies are your priorities.
- She is off your radar.
- That is status quo in the world today.
- Men do not want to be accountable for the children they have sired.

ABANDONMENT

Dad, do you know that child abandonment is a criminal offense? Child abandonment laws vary from state to state, but for the most part it is a felony offense. Abandonment of your child is not just emotional abuse; it is criminal and punishable by law.

While child abandonment typically involves physical abandonment, it includes emotional abandonment, such as when a too-busy or preoccupied parent offers little or no physical contact, such as hugs and kisses, home-cooked meals, times of play and entertainment, or emotional support and presence during traumatizing events. Experiences such as the beginning of school, breakups, health challenges, dating and peer pressures; and important days, such as graduation, marriage and deaths of loved ones—all of these play an integral role in teaching your daughter either to fly or to remain "grounded." Dad, when you are absent and have abandoned your daughter, you hurt her in ways that emotionally debilitate her for a lifetime.

Unfortunately, abandoned children often grow up with low self-esteem, emotional dependency, helplessness, and other issues. These children are referred to in the psychological community as "foundlings;" they have no connection to a nuclear family.

What Constitutes Child Abandonment?

According to Thompson Reuters' FindLaw website, the term "child abandonment" is broadly categorized and used to describe a variety of behaviors. Specific examples of child abandonment vary, but common actions that lead to child abandonment charges may include:

- Leaving a child with another person without provision for the child's support and without meaningful communication with the child for a period of three months;
- Making only minimal efforts to support and communicate with a child;
- Failing for a period of at least six months to maintain regular visitation with a child;
- Failing to participate in a suitable plan or program designed to reunite the parent or guardian with a child;
- Being absent from the home for a period of time that created a substantial risk of serious harm to a child left in the home;
- Failing to respond to a notice of child protective proceedings; or
- Being unwilling to provide care, support, or supervision for the child.[10]

When Dad physically disappears from his children, and he fails to provide necessary care for a child living under his roof, he is guilty of abandonment. This is exactly how social violations occur, i.e., rape, abuse, gang involvement, drug usage and low performance in school; there is no attention or follow up by Dad even though he lives in the same house.

Dad, your business, your absence, your career, or your pure disdain for your family is counted as abandonment, and you have abdicated your emotional responsibility with no justifiable reason. Can you really live with yourself knowing this?

FRIEND OF THE COURT DATA

Across the country, there appears to be a statistical variance between who gets the children in child custody cases: Fathers, Mothers, or both in joint custody. For instance, in Michigan's Wayne County, the disparity is painful. According to a Friend of the Court Statistical Supplement with demographic data from the U.S. Census Bureau, the Friend of the Court recommended that the Mother have custody of the children in 87 percent of the cases; joint custody was advised in 8 percent of the cases, and Fathers were granted custody only 4 percent of the time.11

These numbers are mirrored throughout America. The bottom line is this: *Dads do not parent the majority of the time as sole custodians!* What's wrong with this? The reasons vary, but in many cases, Dads do not *desire* full custody, or they are not financially able to provide what is needed to support decisions in their favor. Other possible factors include lack of employment, lack of permanent, suitable housing, or lack of availability from careers. Or perhaps the desire to be a full-time Dad is sorely lacking. According to

Friend of the Court data, judges across the spectrum find Mothers to be more reliable and available to raise their children.

Dad, if you live at home but are in a failing relationship with your spouse, your daughter sees this and feels the pain of it. You can be an absent Father in the home. Are you estranged from the child within your home? You should commit to your daughter regardless of your relationship with her Mother. You owe it to her, and your failure to invest in your daughter is unjust. It is also just plain cruel. Do you want to harm your daughter? You can do it by doing nothing; just don't invest. You'll break her heart; you'll break her wings and her best chance for success.

Would you go into hiding from your daughter because of her Mother? Do you believe that your daughter needs a Dad as much as she needs a Mother? She does. Dad, she may even need you more. Father-Hunger exists in every girl and woman who hasn't known her Dad's love and its manifestations. Father-Hunger, unfulfilled, will haunt her and keep her from soaring as high as she may desire. I don't want your relationship with your daughter to be forced on you by some tragedy, or by a bitter twist of fate, so take ownership of this vital responsibility. Man up, and make the changes that will benefit both your daughter and you!

Daughters want and need a real relationship with their Fathers, and they want an authentic relationship. In today's society, less and less women have a real relationship with their Fathers. They get a pretense of a relationship. Sometimes they get just the shadow of a relationship when

Dad lives at home, and sometimes they get that from a Dad who provides a lot of huff and puff when he's around but is rarely present.

Pretense of relationship is not healthy. It fosters doubt and anxiety. Like Amy in *Fly Away Home*, your own daughter is not a dummy. Don't underestimate her ability to see that you're too consumed with yourself to be devoted to her. You're not a villain. You are consumed with getting through life like everyone else. But your progeny—your legacy, your lifeline, your children—need you. Your children have to take precedence.

Are you hiding from your daughter? Are you too involved in doing your thing? Working too hard? Are you fearful? What other hindrances keep you from being responsible for your seed? These are all lame excuses, and what is required of you to change can be very simple.

Let's look at some resolutions you can make, and you'll be glad to know that you can overcome any obstacle to honor them.

1. **Communicate**. A daughter wants to hear her Dad's voice. Make the first move. Answer questions honestly, even if the answers may embarrass you. Your transparency with her shows that you are not hiding anything from her. This will make her love you. She is a responder. She will not condemn you; she will love you and learn acceptance.

2. **Change yourself**. Any self-improvement will enrich your relationship with your daughter. Change your reactions and your responses. This will improve the

dialogue between you and your daughter, and give her hope that you are making her a priority. Many think the only way to ameliorate a relationship is for the other person to change. Dad, you change first.

3. **Repair damage quickly**. Realize that there is a conflict and deal with it head-on. Don't argue about it. Resolve it.

4. **Accept responsibility**. Own what you have done or not done. Don't blame anyone else. Admit it to yourself first and then to your daughter. Show your daughter that her hurts and wounds are more important to you than your being right. When you fail to do this, you fail to validate her.

5. **Be an active listener**. Listening without responding says that she's being heard and that her feelings matter. Remember that your daughter operates more in her feelings than in her logic. Don't be protective of yourself, and don't be defensive. *Listen*.

6. **Have realistic goals**. Your relationship with your daughter may not heal overnight. Give it time and be consistent. This relationship is for the long haul; so if it doesn't change immediately, don't abandon the process. Consistency of effort shows your daughter your level of commitment.

If you will invest in your daughter's life now, no matter where she is in her journey, you will dramatically change the outcome of her eventual success. She may have a tough exterior toward you initially, but you don't have to respond in kind. Make the investment of effort on a consistent basis. Take what she allows, but do something. Make time to call her, send a card, or even arrange to see her. Trust me: this matter to her.

You may not understand how much it matters, and you may not see instant results, but you are rebuilding her life's "aircraft" for longer, more purposeful flights. So if you pursue and engage, and recommit to the relationship with your daughter, you will one day stand in view of the runway of her life and watch a takeoff that will astound and reward you with dividends unmatched by wealth or fame.

No more lame excuses, Dad.

No more lame excuses, Dad.

No more lame excuses, Dad.

TAKEAWAYS

- What does an authentic relationship with your daughter look like?
- How much time can you add to your schedule for Daddy-daughter dates?
- What about you needs to change for you to recover your spot in her life?

CHAPTER 4

●●●

Daddy's Issues

**"It took me a really long time to admit that leaving you
and your Mother was a mistake."
– Tom Alden**

Why do men fail? Why do men in general have trouble
with their emotions, communications, and being transparent?
Manifestations of these failures in men have been released
over the course of history. It's been a progression, and the
world has witnessed an acceleration of males'
absence/weakness during the current age. Breakdown of the
family has been unrestrained in the past century; it has
become the norm. What is the result? Modern abdication of
Fatherhood is widespread today and this has some clear-cut
social and emotional components.

Most women I talk to express a common frustration
with their husbands: they won't take responsibility. Another
thing I hear a lot from women is that their men don't have a
plan. Or they are cruel. "He doesn't treat me nicely. He
doesn't talk to me nicely." These are manifestations of

provider-leader abdication, where roles have been switched and responsibility for nurturing has been handed over to the Mothers. What has happened to make men so silent, so soft, or so irresponsible, cold and callous?

The causes are overlapping. I've mentioned that they include fatherlessness, fear, selfishness, and anger with women in general or with their own Mothers. They also include other kinds of anger; a lack of modeling, improper modeling, or negligent modeling; hurts from the past, such as parental abuse; immaturity, impatience, and ignorance that can result in abuse of authority; discouragement and insecurity. Fatherlessness, fear and selfishness are huge issues today.

Fear and anger are emotions that go hand-in-hand, as fear is often the root cause of anger. But don't overlook feelings of inadequacy and feelings of victimization in the family context as other possible reasons for a man's anger, which is often a mask for something else. Men have a hard time with emotions, and anger is the one emotion men seem comfortable owning.

I want you to hear this from a man, though, so you don't think I'm biased, misinformed, or unfair:

Writing for *The Christian Post*, author and speaker Rick Johnson explains,

> *Males are not very adept at understanding their emotions, nor very comfortable dealing with them. Emotions are powerful and often uncontrollable. That's why many males keep such a tight lid on their emotions—once released, they are difficult to predict*

or control and often result in a situation ending in vulnerability. The one emotion, however, that they are relatively comfortable with is that of anger. Anger for many men is an old friend; one they call upon in a variety of circumstances. Like all powerful emotions, it can be used destructively or for good. For instance, anger can be terribly destructive in relationships. … All we need to do is look at the devastation caused to women and children through a man's uncontrolled wrath and anger. Anger can lead to emotional, psychological, and even physical abuse. … Regardless of how it is used, anger is the emotion most familiar to males. [12]

Author Stephen Stosny, Ph.D., writing for *Psychology Today*, says, "Most male anger comes from feeling like a failure as a protector, provider, and sexual-lover."[13] He writes that a feeling of inadequacy may be the root of men becoming emotionally withholding in relationships.

Stosny's theory mirrors the lesson my husband taught from the pulpit one Sunday morning: abdication begets resentment begets abuse.

When a man feels inadequate in the leader-provider role, Stosny says he's likely to become resentful or angry and to portray himself as a victim:

These acute vulnerabilities can be stimulated by the mere unhappiness or displeasure of his wife, even if her distress or negative states have nothing to do with him. And he is likely to blame his sense of failure, and the feelings of inadequacy it stimulates, on her.

Blame gives him status as a victim. Victimhood gives him a temporary sense of self-righteousness, along with a retaliation impulse, which, in turn, stimulates anger.[14]

Both Stosny and Johnson state that men can become addicted to anger. Stosny writes that it can cause men to develop depression:

The adrenalin rush of anger, like any other amphetamine effect, always crashes into some level of depression, at least in the form of self-doubt and energy depletion. He then uses a low-grade resentment to militate out of depressed mood—to gain temporary confidence and energy. Resentment keeps him partially aroused most of the time and highly susceptible to angry outbursts. The excess adrenalin and cortisol in his bloodstream make it hard for him to sleep and more difficult to concentrate when awake. Often tired and distracted, he needs more anger for energy, focus, and motivation. He gets caught on a recurring rollercoaster of resentment-anger-depression-resentment-anger-depression.
Chronic blame keeps him mired in victim-identity, which continually reignites the cycle. If he allows himself to realize that he may be a victimizer, he sinks lower.

Once this pattern becomes habituated, the content—what makes him angry—is no longer important, as he will look for anything to give him the adrenalin shot he needs. He becomes a kind of anger-

junkie, in search of blame to get his fix. He lives predominantly in two emotional states, either buzzing along with some form of low-grade anger or plodding ahead in a mildly depressed mood. His life becomes a joyless drive to get things done.[15]

Anger may manifest itself in outbursts, or it may fester. Men who are trying to behave in a way considered civil by society may hold in their anger and meditate on it, which may lead to long-term disassociation from the family, even within the home. Or it may manifest outwardly. Sometimes feelings of inadequacy in men cause outwardly expressed anger with a purpose of covering over the inadequacy. Rick Johnson writes:

You'll notice that nearly all males will react with anger when they become overly frustrated or are hurt emotionally. ... Anger is often a secondary emotion used by males to cover or mask other emotions. For instance, certain emotions, such as fear, anxiety, vulnerability, or distress often produce a feeling of humiliation in males. Males consider humiliation a weakness. Remember, for most males, to show weakness is to be vulnerable and open to criticism. To be vulnerable is an invitation to be attacked. But anger is a defense against attack and may even be a weapon to attack others. Very angry men and boys are seldom messed with, even by bullies.

Rather than feel humiliated by these "unmanly" emotions, many males instinctively and automatically use anger to cover those feelings. Even pain (physical or psychological) can be covered by anger. Notice how most males react when they hit their thumb with a hammer. They'd rather get mad than cry. Most men also get angry rather than depressed or hysterical when faced with an emotional crisis in a relationship. Again, this is a protective mechanism for their fragile egos; egos that are covering secretly ingrained feelings of inadequacy and incompetence.[16]

So we see that fear is indeed a root of men's abdication of responsibility to Father. Fear makes fragile men. Fear of making mistakes, fear of failure, and fear of emotions all cause men to abdicate family responsibility. Men hate failure. They abdicate because they fear failure. Fear causes men to procrastinate to the point of neglect. And neglect—failure to do what you know you must do—brings out resentment. The resentment accelerates neglect, and ultimately the neglect becomes abuse. Absolutely, fear causes irresponsibility, which leads to loathing and harm. It's an absolutely perverted progression of cause and effect.

Another form of fear is insecurity about one's own worth as a human and as a Father: "How could I ever be able to Father this child?"

We've discussed the notion that men have trouble with emotions. Even a man who's not emotionally immature can fear his daughter's own emotions, particularly as she grows into a young woman. Some Fathers are unsure how to deal with their daughters' emotions on top of their own. A daughter brings out hard emotion in a man. A daughter will make him feel something. A daughter will make him cry. And she can make him hurt and feel pain as a Father.

Fear of arousal is another issue. Some men are just not comfortable with their own emotions or their own feelings about their sexuality and their daughters' own sexuality. Sometimes, loving their daughters opens men up to arousal, because they've never been able to differentiate between erotic love and selfless love.

There's hope, Dad.

You must learn to own your anger. You must identify its source, determine whether it is rooted in fear or something else, and then you can learn to respond appropriately. Channeled productively, anger can motivate you to achievement.

Did you know that a Father's feelings of inadequacy are God-designed? Just as your daughter needs you and feels Father-Hunger without your presence, you will feel the deep gnawing that you're outside of God's intent, as long as you're not taking care of your daughter as you're designed to do. Are you a leader-provider? Do you feel angry? Find out the root. Work to overcome it. Are you fearful? Then get some help to see what is driving your fears. Therapy is your friend; start with some one-on-one sessions to get a real handle on your emotions. Often, your counselor will want to know about your own childhood.

PAPA WAS A ROLLING STONE

When we look at the life of a "rolling stone" type of Dad, we typically see:

- A lack of modeling.
- Promiscuity.
- Lack of commitment.
- Sexual perversion.
- Instability.
- Poverty.

Sometimes a man's abdication of responsibility is due to the fact that he wasn't Fathered adequately himself. Your own Dad may have been totally absent, for various reasons, or he might have been absent emotionally, even though you lived under his roof. Either way, you will suffer from Father-Hunger. Men who didn't have a Father in their lives during their childhood can let that childhood become an excuse for not being good Fathers to their own children.

If your Father was not present, you had to get your modeling from someone or somewhere. That might have been your brother, your classmates and peers, or someone else in the home, including your Mother. Or it might have been a Stepfather or a Grandfather. But if your Father was at home, you most likely got your model of what a man is from him.

If your Father didn't provide for the family financially, if he didn't invest time in you personally, if he didn't show respect to others, if he was prone to outbursts and impulse decisions, if he passed blame on to others, if he was overbearing, if he was dismissive of you or invalidated you, if he broke promises, was late, was broke, if he lied or cheated or made excuses, if he failed to express his love, then you suffered from a lack of proper modeling. You're lucky if you did have a nurturer who was able to model appropriate parenting. But if not, your own Father-Hunger is likely a hindrance to your relationship with your daughter.

Men with Father-Hunger are like wounded eagles when they're young. Watch them and you can see that these men have their wings, but they don't trust them to fly and they never provide the confidence or the wings their daughters need.

Author Joseph Mattera says Fatherlessness births insecurity and inferiority in men early in life. "They never fully trust their abilities and hence they don't always trust others around them. This sense of inferiority causes them to try to hide their low self-esteem by projecting a machismo persona full of confidence."[17] Mattera says the lack of trust in authority figures causes Fatherless men to become fiercely independent:

> *Some men who have experienced Fatherlessness have a hard time inwardly submitting to any form of spiritual authority, even if they outwardly attempt to do so. They mostly make their own decisions without getting real counsel, and if they do get counsel, they will ultimately do what they want anyway because they don't believe anyone fully looks out for their interests.*[18]

Men with Father-Hunger have insecurities that make them strive for their Father's approval. They constantly compare themselves to other men, which causes conflicts, and they may be selfishly ambitious. Mattera notes:

> *Many Fatherless men are psychologically living their lives to prove themselves to their Fathers (whether alive or dead) that they are valuable, that they are worthy of their Fathers' love. The interesting thing about this is, they may even hate their Fathers emotionally but not be aware that they are emotionally geared to finally secure the approval of their Fathers.*[19]

Men who lacked Dads in their youth, Mattera says, have feelings of loneliness and emptiness. "Many Fatherless men are always striving, never satisfied, and never happy. Thus they are always looking to a better future and never enjoy the present."[20]

Meanwhile, they suffer from an inability to relate to their own kids. It's devastating.

Dr. O'Shan D. Gadsden concurs with Mattera that Father-Hunger affects the male's self-worth and forces him to create his own notions of masculinity and appropriate masculine behavior. Gadsden says that in his own life growing up without a Father, he fabricated distorted depictions of patriarchal masculinity, romanticized and adopted from the media and popular culture.

> *After years of personal therapy and metaphysical practice, I have become intimately aware of how my 'Father lack' affected my ability to*

feel safe in the world, to take myself seriously, and to demand the best from myself and others. Additionally, this Father lack negatively affected my connections and ability to navigate the emotional world of romantic relationships. ... I realized that my Father lack greatly influenced the way in which I communicated to and behaved toward the women in my life. I had to resolve my neediness for connection as well as my veiled hostility toward the women I felt held the power to either grant love to me or deny me its access. This cognitive and emotional dissonance was greatly related to unresolved issues connected to my Father lack. There were times I felt helpless, fearing that I could not and would not measure up to expectations of my romantic interest. I realized, that although the other came with her own developmental history that impacted mine; at the heart of the matter was my own split-off and unhealed internal world. I journeyed daily with a grave sense of emotional and spiritual impotence, the feeling that despite all my external accomplishments, I could not and would not ever be good enough.[21]

Dad, don't use excuses, such as being emotionally non-committed, manipulative, and excessively angry, to hide your fear of parenting.

Men with Father-Hunger often wind up in relationships with women whom they would normally never get into relationship with, had they had good Fathering. Often these girlfriends are older, settled, more mature, and more secure. These men are looking for self-validation, self-esteem, and other traits they didn't get from a Father who was present. These men have never learned consistency and structure from their Fathers; they often turn to older women, who are mature enough to take on a type of surrogate Fathering figure, even if they don't realize this is what they are doing. It's a far cry from having your Father invest in you, but it's as close as many men get to the security that the Father was ordained to provide.

Sometimes men without Fathers do one of two things: they clump or they isolate. They clump, as in gangs, or they isolate as loners. They don't commit easily, nor do they commit well. Their Father-Hunger drives them, and you can tell that by the way these men overcompensate if they get married and have children. Sometimes they overcompensate with structure, or with discipline or the lack thereof. They don't know how to Father because there was no imprint from a male in their own life, so they wing it. While some men will get the help they need from relationships, reading, or research, most men will try to master this art of parenting without any outside resources.

I know a member of the clergy, a big, strong, beautiful man with a great family. He's successful on the outside but he's a broken man. He searches for affluence, affirmation and importance; but he has social challenges and issues, and deficits in relating to people. He prefers to be isolated with just those he knows well and trusts.

Why? It's simple: fear. He had been abandoned as a young child and was often lied to and disappointed. He remembers many incidents of his Father not coming to see him and his brothers, as they sat patiently waiting. The Father never showed up, and this man with Father-Hunger always feels the need to overcompensate. In every relationship, he must be in control in order to validate and protect himself from ever being left again.

After all these years, he is still afraid of loss and rejection, so he eventually loses everyone he gets involved with in his effort to keep them, or he pushes them away for fear of them leaving him first. So you know what's happening: people do leave him, because the rage that accompanies the control, the jealousy and cynicism that are co-joined to his leadership make people so uncomfortable that they have to depart from him in order to live.

Other men, who may stay in relationships out of fear-based loyalty, lose a little of themselves over time, but because they suffer from Father-Hunger, their attachment feeds their own need.

If you lacked a Dad, don't be discouraged. You can still be a great Father to your children, especially to your daughter, and you can launch her into greatness. Even if you've known Father-Hunger for your entire life, you can overcome. There is help for you to prevail over your own Fatherlessness. Let me share how I know this.

My Father, my phenomenal Dad, didn't have a Father. He grew up as an orphan in Atlanta, Georgia. He didn't really know his family and I never met any of his family members. He told us his story. He knew his Mom, but not his Dad; he was put into his aunt's home; and from time to time, other relatives would take him in. I never met my paternal

Grandfather, so I know my Dad missed some parenting in his life. But he didn't let it limit him from having a great family with great children.

And you don't have to, either. I believe that because of what happened to him—having been an orphan and having known what it means to be a child really alone—he was determined not to let that happen with his own children. He worked really hard to have a stable environment with my Mother at the helm of the home, and all of my siblings in tow. Mr. Lewis was known to be a stellar example of husband and Father in our community. I think that when he met my Mom, he just said, "I must get this right." I don't know what happened, and I don't know how he did it.

He was a man, just an ordinary man with a difficult past. He wasn't a loud guy and he wasn't a Type A personality, but he was a strong man. He meant what he said and he said what he meant, and he was willing to stand, even if he had to stand by himself, in order to build a strong family.

Another successful man who knew great Father-Hunger is President Barack Obama. His Dad was estranged from the family when Barack was very young, yet he became commander-in-chief of the United States, leader of the free world. He is a great success and a rock star to the black community. He had Father-Hunger, so what has he done? He has become a phenomenal Father, a great husband, and a beloved leader, just like my Father did.

In the movie *Fly Away Home*, the Dad, Mr. Alden, was not a great Dad during the marriage or after the divorce. But he finally realizes he can turn that around and have a great relationship with his daughter. By acknowledging his mistakes, he endears her to trust him and together they become a great family.

Dad, you don't have to ruin the rest of your life because the first part of your life was far from perfect. Regroup! Reposition yourself! Reengage in the fight for Fathering well. You can be a great man, husband and Father; if you will invest in yourself, great results will follow. Your family needs you to be the "best you" that you can be. So move ahead; overcome your issues, and stop blaming everyone else for your lack of discipline and commitment. Get on with the future by leaving the past. You are alive! You made it out! You survived and now you must change the outcome of what appeared to be a fatal ending. Forgive, release and let go of the people who disappointed you. Why live the rest of your life hating it and transferring that hatred of life to your children? You, Dad, have the power to raise excellent children and excellent citizens who will make contributions in their lifetimes that cannot be erased.

Love yourself enough to get professional help if needed; read the books; take the parenting classes; seek spiritual advisement; and find mentors who can make impartations as needed. The best years are ahead of you, if you are willing to make the hard choices and changes. You will be so proud of your children, and they will be proud to call you Dad.

Emotional Disconnected Dads

So what happens when Dad is in the home but is less than able to be what his family needs him to be? Maybe he suffers from:

- Hurts from the past.
- Abuse of authority.
- A selfish Father figure.
- Absence of affirmation and affection.

My husband has a story about his Dad that told me a lot about his upbringing. His Dad was not an affectionate man, and he was a very strict disciplinarian with his thirteen children. One day while my husband was growing up, his Dad went to give one of his sisters a good spanking, and my husband, a teenager, ran and jumped on his Father's back, trying to constrain him.

His Father said, "Are you on my back?"

"Yes, sir!"

"What are you doing on my back?"

"I don't want you to whip Sister!"

"Fine. Then I'm going to whip you."

My husband said that's the worst beating he ever got.

Now you would think my husband had done the right thing, the honorable thing, right? Wrong. While you may not agree with his Father's treatment of his children, you must know that this was not my husband's responsibility to correct. He overstepped his boundaries in his Father's home, and he dishonored his Father. Even though the Dad may have abused his power as Father, it was not the child's role to correct his Father. There was never any discussion about this event and no affection shown afterward. So, when negative modeling is present, the children, even when grown, have a very difficult mental mindset to change. They suffer from that upbringing; the abuse of authority, bad memories, lack of affection, and absence of positive affirmation create Father-Hunger, even when a Father is in the home.

WHEN DAD IS BAD

Abuse of authority plays out in two ways: A man may have suffered from abuse of authority in his childhood, at the hands of his Father, which causes Father-Hunger. Meanwhile, a man who has a distorted definition of manhood may act out through the abuse of his authority and be a terror to his own family.

Men for centuries have also used religion to support their lack of Fathering skills. It's easy to do: It happens any time a family leader quits being "leader-provider" and becomes the "boss." While serving others, he uses the cloak of spirituality to cover his own lack of confidence at being the man he really needs to be in his own home. This man wants his spouse to provide the money, the nurturing, the emotional support, and the protection component for the family. While the husband is supposed to be the household leader and the lead provider, through distorted views of gender roles concerning male superiority, he uses religious mandates like a rubber mallet across the heads of his family members to support his own abdication of his Father role. When Fathering goes bad, everyone suffers. In many cases where a Father is absent, Father-Hunger is easy to recognize, but when the Father is present, yet still unable to Father, the children will inevitably be neglected. They will grow up "emotionally immature" in many areas unless there is a strong Mother who can maintain balance and training for the children.

NARCISSISM

Your own Father's narcissism is another form of abuse that can cause you to fail in your role as family patriarch.

I know a man who is forty-five but still a boy, and he has deep Father-Hunger. He's been adrift since the day he left his Father's home, rootless, because he lacked nurturing. His Father was a narcissist, and his Mother was the codependent in charge of keeping the narcissist happy; she was there to protect him. Rather than nurture the son, whose intelligence was evident in his childhood, she worked to protect the Father from scrutiny. She worked to indulge the Father in his interests, leaving little time for either parent to cultivate the son. They found out when he was in elementary school that his abilities were far higher than his production, but they were not equipped to deal with the idea that something was amiss in the home.

The narcissist lacks awareness of other people's needs, even in his own family. The narcissist ignores personal boundaries and has a sense of entitlement, particularly among his family, such as a king in his palace. The narcissist lacks empathy, and is arguably unfit for parenthood; but he nevertheless has children in the blind conviction that they enlarge and perpetuate his own worth.

The narcissistic parent either "engulfs" or "ignores." The engulfer sees his children as extensions of himself and is preoccupied with how his children perform and how they appear. The engulfing narcissist may become abusive when a child does not fulfill his expectations and desires, which are always rooted in the narcissist's self-importance. The engulfer micromanages and invades privacy. The engulfing narcissist believes his children exist for his own sake.

The children of narcissistic "ignorers" don't get such overbearing attention, or much at all. They usually grow up feeling unloved and mistreated, and they have inadequacy issues that cause them to struggle to form meaningful relationships.

Self-centeredness causes the narcissist to take advantage of his children. While he may be charismatic, he responds poorly to criticism, distancing himself from, or becoming irate and vengeful toward, those who shine a light on his flaws. Ultimately, a child of a narcissist can't get his emotional needs fulfilled. The Father meets his child's needs only when doing so fulfills his own needs. His failure to recognize that others have needs causes the narcissistic Father to treat his family as personal servants. The abuse is subtle, but the damage occurs nonetheless.

Psychiatrist and author Mark Banschick writes about such damage in an article for *Psychology Today:*

> *Narcissistic parents often damage their children. For example, they may disregard boundaries, manipulate*

their children by withholding affection (until they perform), and neglect to meet their children's needs because their needs come first. Because image is so important to narcissists, they may demand perfection from their children. The child of a narcissist Father can, in turn, feel a pressure to ramp up [the child's] talents, looks, smarts or charisma. It can cost them if they fulfill their Dad's wishes—and it can cost them if they fail. No winning here.[22]

Banschick says the children of a narcissistic Father feel as if they can never measure up: Dad either was so competitive that he played to win even with his children, or was so into himself that he didn't pay attention to his children at all. Either way, the children usually feel empty or second-rate. The male child may become a narcissist himself or feel inadequate for life. No matter the outcome, the male child of a narcissist has Father-Hunger, and he is at risk of failing to nurture his own children adequately.

Psychiatrists agree that the adult child of a narcissistic parent probably needs professional therapy and may be healthier if he leaves the relationship with the narcissistic parent behind. Or he can get extensive counseling over a long period of time to restore what has been stripped.

THE MAN IN THE MIRROR

- Self-absorption
- Selfishness
- Sex and the selfish man

Take a hard look at your priorities. Are you self-absorbed? Are you selfish? Could you be a narcissist? Narcissism in your Dad can be passed on to you. And your narcissism is not just a potential detriment to your daughter's sense of worth; it's a life killer. Banschick talks about the effect of a Father's narcissism on daughters:

> *Daughters of narcissistic Fathers often describe feeling "unsatiated" when it comes to getting what they needed from their Fathers. They never got enough and would have to compete with siblings for time with Dad. When you were a young child, Dad would comment on how beautiful you were. But as you grew older, he would rarely miss out on commenting about your weight and attitude. You probably carry these concerns into adulthood, even if you found success. With a Dad like this, it's never enough … you often feel vulnerable and worried that you'll be dumped for someone else. Anxiously avoiding commitment or taking on the narcissistic role are both natural ways to keep relationships safe; it's understandable and self-protective. (But, you lose.)*[23]

A daughter needs her Dad's adoration; it validates her and helps her internalize her specialness. Healthy Fathers should give their girls that gift.

Narcissism in its extreme forms is a mental disorder. Self-absorption is much the same as narcissism, but it lacks the mental disorder stigma. In fact, self-absorption is one of the traits of narcissism.

Matt Moody, a social psychologist, points to definitions of selfishness: 1) focus upon one's own advantage to the exclusion of regard for others, and 2) lacking consideration for others; concerned with one's own personal profit or pleasure. He defines narcissism as "excessive interest in one's own physical appearance; extreme selfishness with a grandiose view of one's own talents and attractiveness, having a consistent craving for admiration."

Moody writes, "For most people, the two words might be used interchangeably, but there *is* a salient difference between selfishness [and] narcissism. Selfishness is a word that applies to most human beings some of the time, whereas narcissism is a kind of consistent selfishness that is more pronounced."[24]

Nevertheless, simple, pure selfishness is another huge reason why men have abdicated their responsibility to their offspring. Selfishness manifests in a spectrum. It can be blatant and it can be subtle. Selfishness has a root in pride, and pride is hard to see in oneself. So we don't always know we are selfish. We don't always admit it.

The first step to overcoming your own selfishness, Dad, is to admit that you are selfish. Then start investing in others, with your family and your children coming first. This investment of your time in your daughters is more valuable than your investment in tangible items, such as expensive clothes, automobiles, and expendable goods. Money is not a suitable substitute for time; neither will it empower your daughter to soar to her greatest potential.

SEXUAL DEVIANCE AND SUPERIORITY

Talk show host Maury Povich has those "Is This Your Child?" episodes, and I saw one the other day. A young man found out that he had fathered a child, and he was stupefied. In his mind, his seed didn't have worth. In his value system, his seed had no consequence other than being a byproduct of physical pleasure. This is a prevailing issue of men in our current age.

Maury asked the young man, "Now that you know the child is yours, what are you going to do?" The young man responded, "I'm going to do the right thing." And I said to the television, "You don't even know what's right." This proves my theory that sex is a dangerous thing in the hands of the immature male. Sex does not belong in the hands of children.

Men don't value sexual intercourse for its original purpose, which was to create the family. When sex is not an act of thoughtfulness, or an act of responsibility, it becomes selfish passion and produces children for whom no one wants to assume the responsibility of training and Fathering. Both sons and daughters then suffer from the "spirit of the orphan;" unwanted, unprepared for, unloved, and positioned for failure. Sadly, cultures of Fatherless children are becoming the norm. It is inconceivable that we have so many women who find out who the Father of their child is on a national television show.

When sex is taken outside of marriage, intercourse becomes nothing more than a simple joystick and extension of the male ego, affirming the male's self-worth and sense of belonging. The female victim of such a male exposes herself to the emotional pain of sex without the security of love, and with no provision for her or their child. Before the child can get started in life, he/she is already severely handicapped and must live with the stigma of being "illegitimate." A daughter in this environment is sorely displaced and feels the need to imitate her Mother, who may have several children, all by different Dads. Hence the cycle continues and gains momentum. Countless children, the majority of them daughters, are born without Fathers. The men never intended to have influence in their daughters' lives, so these girls are already behind the eight ball.

I sometimes teach a concept called "phallus perception" or "penis power." P-h-a-l-l-u-s is the penis. Men think of it as so powerful, as a scepter of power, but it does not represent power; the penis represents responsibility. An orphaned male who has had no Fathering thinks that his penis is the organ of manhood, and as soon as the young male is able, he wants sexual freedom. The expression of this immaturity creates more and more Father-Hunger, by creating more and more children, whom the young male is totally unable to raise. Orphan men create orphan children. Men without self-worth and men without good examples of Fatherhood are innumerous in today's culture.

So what about the children? What about the byproducts of this trend? What happens to the family unit that is now raised by a single parent, usually without enough resources? The average teenage Dad doesn't have a job. He cannot cook; he cannot pay the bills. Who will be the Father figure for these children?

I think we need to start teaching our sons about the power of sperm, and to teach this at an earlier age. That sex is not just pleasure; it is responsibility. It's not power; it's responsibility that will change your life forever.

While in Florida during a Father's Day event years back, I taught a lesson called "The Value of the Seed." Men think it's just two teaspoons of fluid that proves the extent of their excitement, but this fluid carries life for which they are responsible. You sired a child from your body, and the responsibility of the seed is yours and always will be. The sexual climax is only seconds long, but the consequences are life changing and long-lasting. The sexual encounter may be a pleasure "moment," but parenting is a covenant in which the two people now become responsible for a child, for a couple of decades at minimum.

Dad, it's time to restore order by doing the right things for the right outcomes, by overcoming any and all of these issues to become the Father your children need. If you have any of these Daddy issues, you must confront them; self-image and self-worth issues, control and anger issues, and all sexual issues can be overcome.

Commit to being a man of purity with all the women who encounter you. No woman should anticipate that you would take advantage of her in any way. Rape, molestation, incest, pornography, promiscuity, and all other sexual violations must cease.

Sexual immorality disrupts the order of civilization, the order of the family, and the order of life as we know it should be. *Sexual manipulation is wrong*. Sexual superiority over women is wrong. Sexual impropriety is wrong; it creates a culture of disengaged fathers and children. Poverty, prostitution, crime, and more, ensue from it and dominate our court systems, school systems, church systems, and economic systems, all because of carelessness with the male seed.

Men, don't produce a child that you have no intention of being responsible for. Admit it when you have made this mistake, and seek to correct the wrong. If you have a child you are not supporting financially, change that—now! If you have a child you do not visit because of issues with the Mother, change that—now! If you are in the home with your children, but are emotionally absent, change that—now! If you have gone through a divorce and do not have custody in your favor, go back to court and rework the judgment of the court.

Do everything you must do to improve yourself so you can be the Dad your daughter needs for the rest of her life.

TAKEAWAYS

- Examine your childhood and present life. What can you do immediately so that you do not perpetuate harmful cycles?
- What is your biggest issue and what can you do to change it?
- Can you forgive your Father for being absent? If not, can you find someone who can help you come to that place of forgiveness?

CHAPTER 5

● ● ●

I Built You Your Own Wings.

"Suppose I were to build another aircraft and teach Amy to fly."

Fathers who want the best for their daughters do more than just provide security and enforce boundaries. They make investments in their daughter's future gifts and purpose. They sacrifice to push their daughters forward.

In *Fly Away Home*, Amy Alden took responsibility for her clutch of goose eggs, and Thomas Alden became responsible for them, too. He was not hands-on; he let her do the nurturing. The geese were his daughter's, but she was his, so the geese became part of his charge. Rather than working through the day-to-day care of the geese, he saw the bigger picture.

As soon as Amy's Father became aware that the geese were in peril if they stayed at his farm through the winter, he began working to protect them. He was not as blatantly concerned about the geese as Amy was; he was acting on the geese's behalf for the purpose of investing in his daughter. He was striving to be a phenomenal Father.

That's important: he didn't just take responsibility for his seed. He invested in her. He did more than pay bills, provide a roof and get her on the bus for school. He built her an ultra-light aircraft and taught her to fly it so that her dreams wouldn't die.

Thomas Alden was an idea guy, an artist and a dreamer, and his solution was unprecedented. He had a passion and a vision, and skill. His solution was to guide the geese on a 1,000-mile migration flight from central Canada to the coast of North Carolina. His big idea came to fruition because he was interested in his daughter's welfare.

He knew he couldn't get the birds to follow him, and he knew she couldn't fly his aircraft. His passion was his little plane. His vision was to build Amy her own airplane.

Fathers must build their daughters' identities and dreams, their vehicles of movement and motion and growth. They build their daughters' infrastructure for life.

I love the parallel between my destiny, nurtured by my Father, and Amy's destiny, nurtured by her Father. Amy's Father built her the plane, a beautiful plane, one that she would never be ashamed of. He took his own investment and used it as a resource to make her dream come to fruition.

Like Thomas Alden, my own Dad didn't know that his fulfillment of purpose would be his greatest achievement, his legacy. As their circumstances played out, both Thomas Alden and Henry Nathaniel Lewis Sr. discovered that their calling—their dabbling—was higher than they could have imagined. They both discovered that their legacy was in their daughters. They eventually realized that they would start something and that their daughters would fulfill it.

Legacies begin at home with a little flock of babies. For Thomas and Amy Alden, it was baby geese; for Henry Lewis Sr., it was his daughter, Corletta J. Vaughn, a different kind of flock.

The parallel between my life and Amy's makes me smile, too. Thomas was an artist, deliberate and laid back. My Father was methodical, slow to act. Amy and I are both driven. We set goals, we act, and we don't give up.

The moment Amy stumbled upon a clutch of eggs at the edge of her Daddy's property, she went into action. Something *inside* her made her act. Her act was instinctive and innate. It was the Mother in her. She went right into action, saving lives. It's worth noting that when she took up those eggs, she had no idea of the monumental task that lay ahead. Can I point out that the little girl was already working against the odds just to have a successful outcome?

The geese all hatched, and she zealously raised them. She became attached. Meanwhile, her Father did some research on geese, and he saw that he had to help her adjust to their needs. He was able to help her see past her wishes to focus on the greater need of her responsibility.

The parallel of this movie to my own life is so beautiful. Thomas Alden dabbled in flying tiny planes. But he did not make it his passion until he saw that his daughter could make a difference if he would teach her how to fly a small plane herself. My Daddy made baseball and ministry his passions. And he taught me both. Thomas Alden knew his daughter was uniquely positioned to save some birds. My Daddy came to understand that I too had a destiny: to set "caged" people free.

Thomas Alden made his living as an industrial artist. He built large-scale projects that took weeks and months to complete. He had a full-scale working model of NASA's lunar lander, and he cherished it. Somebody had asked him to sell it, but he said, no, I'm keeping that. But the geese were growing up, and they would need to fly south as winter approached.

When Alden realized he could not fly the ducks south himself because they would not follow him, and that they would only follow Amy, he came up with the idea that his daughter could lead them if she had the right resources. He knew then that she would need her own plane. And he knew that it would require resources. So he sold the lunar lander and built Amy her own plane. Selling his prized possession did not leave him bitter; it left him beaming with pride and anticipation.

That's what Fathers do.

Look at this closely: he had a little plane that he was playing with, a plane of his own. It was his hobby and passion. But his plane wouldn't fit Amy. Now he knew she was ready for her own plane, one that was fitted perfectly to suit her; one that would suit the task at hand, her vision, her purpose, to keep her safe for future flights. It was a better craft than the one he had built for his own pleasure. He even customized Amy's aircraft so that it looked like the assignment at hand. Since she would be leading her geese south, Dad knew the craft would have to capture the geese's attention. So he designed it to look like a big goose. The design showed that he perceived the gravity of Amy's assignment; he didn't want her to lose the geese. He didn't want her to fail.

When I was a little girl, my Daddy taught me about the value of money.

He was a beauty/barber supply salesman, so he always had cash. At night, he would come home and put all his change in his top dresser drawer. There had to be three or four hundred dollars' worth of change in that drawer.

One evening, when I was about seven-years-old, he called to me, "Come here."

I went over to him at the change drawer, and he said, "All this is yours. Can you count?"

"Yes, sir."

"OK, take it out. Let's see if you can count."

My Mama had been teaching me how to count, so I knew how to count quarters and dimes and nickels and pennies; there were no dollars, just change. He watched me count some out, and then he said, "OK, you can count. Everything in this drawer is yours. All I ask you to do is, when you take something out, leave a note."

"OK," I replied.

I was scared at first to take any money. Every night he would put more change in. At the end of the week, he said, "Have you used any of your money?"

"No, sir."

"Why not? It's yours. Where's your little purse? When you go to school, do you take your purse, your bag, and your lunch box?"

"Yes, sir, all three."

"Put your money in one of them. Don't ever leave the house without money," he said. "You're a young girl. Always have money."

He was imprinting. And the imprint went beyond just, "Money's important."

When my sister came—I begged God for a sister—we were eight years apart. When I was about eleven, she was three, toddling around. She was my baby and I was her hero. When she started going to school at age five, my Daddy told her, "Go ask your sister for your money; don't ask me. Ask your sister."

He wanted to teach me responsibility for her. Daddy told her, "Your sister got all the money that you will need."

I think he knew that at some point in life he wouldn't be here, so he was doing more than I could see. In telling her that, he was telling me, "Take responsibility. Watch over your siblings. Be a good steward. Share."

She would come to me for money, and she would say, "Daddy said for you to give me this money."

I would say, "How much do you need?" We would sit down together and I would teach her how to count. I taught her with that same drawer full of money that my Dad gave me. I told her, "Now don't you go in the drawer without me, but everything in there is ours, and I will share with you."

She said, "Oh, OK."

"Because if you go in without me, you're stealing it; but if you ask, I'll give you anything."

One day she said, "I need ten dollars."

"For what, what do you need ten dollars for?"

"I'm going on a field trip. I need money for food, and to get myself something."

We went in the drawer, and I gave her ten dollars. I gave it to her all in quarters, and I got out a bag and wrapped it up for her.

My Dad was teaching me to copy him, to take responsibility and to share.

He was building my plane all along. By putting money in that drawer, taking me on sales calls, setting boundaries—he was building my plane. By giving me responsibility for my siblings, he was still the pilot, but he was letting me operate the controls. Launching his legacy, he was flying beside me. And by standing up for me and championing my purpose, he was making sure that I could fly on my own, even in the "fog" of life.

This is significant for me. When my Father began the family enterprise, he made sure his vision included me. This goes back to the beginning, when he was told that he was to teach me to walk in his steps. He matured and discovered that life wasn't all about baseball. That might have been a blow, because he might have been thinking that his daughter would become one of the first female professional baseball players.

A Father instills incredible confidence in his daughter when he prepares for her future and realizes that her accomplishments may outweigh his own.

Amy's plane was bigger than her Father's. And Amy's plane was built for distance; it was built to lead others. Her Dad's plane could fly only a certain distance before it would inevitably come down to the ground. He tried several times to fly a greater distance and never really succeeded. He had a small plane with a rudimentary design, but it gave him the practice he needed to build his daughter a much sleeker vehicle to take her into her future.

Father, you must realize that when you build your daughter's plane, it should be bigger, better, more refined, and without the same mistakes that yours had. When you're building your daughter's future, she must know that what you see for her is something much bigger, with a larger span, for greater distances, greater speed, and a higher altitude than what you have achieved for yourself. She will do more than you. She will be greater than you. She will go farther than you, but remember that you built the plane. So the honor is still yours. Never be jealous of your daughter. Never be jealous of her successes. Never fade into the background, and never become anonymous. Your daughter's success is still your victory.

TAKEAWAYS

- What do you see in your daughter and her future?
- How can you "build her an airplane" that is better than yours?
- What is it that holds you back from helping her to fulfill her destiny? Whatever it is, you need to deal with it. Will you?

CHAPTER 6

●●●

Crashing Early

A Daughter Is Going to Make Mistakes.

Your daughter is going to make mistakes no matter how well you parent her. You've made them; she's going to make them, too, even if you're a phenomenal Father, and even if you're not.

In *Fly Away Home*, before Thomas Alden taught Amy to fly, he told her about his idea to lead her geese to their winter migration. She was opposed, but after she considered the alternatives—clipping the birds' wings or having them confiscated—she warmed to the idea. Without her Father's oversight, she climbed into his plane while it was still warm from a previous flight. Dad was distracted and not paying attention. Amy started the little plane and it took off. She crashed it before it could leave the ground. Though she could have been killed, she was hurt badly.

I marvel that we don't all get killed. Daughters sometimes do stupid things. Sometimes they have no idea of the dangers ahead of them, or sometimes they perceive dangers but think they're mature enough to avoid them on their own.

How many girls move too fast into decisions that should be made later in life? How many girls get married before they are ready because they want a man in their life? How many girls get involved in early activities because of peer pressure, smoking, drugs, alcohol, or even promiscuity? How many girls are involved in other wayward adventures?

In every girl, there is a desire to see where boundaries begin and end. How far can I go before I crash? How many drinks can I take before I pass out? How many cigarettes can I smoke before they damage me? How many times can I sneak out of the house before I get caught? How many relationships do I involve myself in with people whom my parents will not approve of, if they found out? Girls are just as adventurous as boys; gender does not define adventure.

Some girls are covert about their adventurous natures, so their silence is in no way a barometer for the parents to gauge their child's appetite for what is forbidden. They may be quiet. They may do what they do in secret. They may do it when no one is watching or listening. They ponder in their heads and seek after adventure on their computers or iPads, because they desire the thrill of adventure just as much as the precocious child whom everyone is watching.

It's impossible to always watch your daughter every moment of the day, so it is vitally important that you give guidelines early on and that you are available emotionally, physically, and financially. When she crosses those boundaries—and she will, often—you must provide a way to repair the things that were broken during her premature, untimely, unscheduled flights.

While I was very young, my Dad allowed me to drive; I was actually just eight-years-old. And from the time I was five, I would sit in his lap and hold the steering wheel. One day while my Dad wasn't watching, I grabbed my sister, and we jumped in the car with the keys. I started the car and backed it out, then drove it down the alley. My sister and I were screaming with glee as we turned around in an empty field, and we were going really fast. My Dad was away at work, and my Mother, who worked in a home business, was completely distracted. Neither had a clue that I would jump into the car with the keys and take the joyride of my life.

After about ten or fifteen minutes of having a wonderful ride in my Dad's new car, I decided it was time to return the car to its parking space in our garage and make sure it looked like I had done nothing.

I made a fast, sharp turn, but it was too tight, so I literally tore the entire wall off the garage. Oh, boy! I had crashed early.

My sister was screaming, "Oh, my God, we're going to die! Look what you did to the garage!" All of a sudden, it was me, just me, who had done it. My sister had wanted to go with me, but she now took absolutely no responsibility. She ran from the car and into the house to my Mother, who was in her beauty salon with a client. "Mom, I gotta whisper you something," my sister said. She told my Mother of my encounter with the garage, and I was terrified; not only had I demolished the west wall of the garage, but my Daddy's brand new car was damaged, with scratches, dings and bangs I didn't have the resources to repair.

I knew my Mother was going to tell my Father; that's how it was in our home. So I sat in that car for what seemed like hours before I went in to face my fate. If the crash hadn't killed me, my Mother would.

When I walked in, my Mother was very concerned about my well-being. She said, "Are you OK?"

I began to cry. "I'm OK, but please don't tell Dad," I begged.

She said, "You're going to be all right. We have insurance. We'll fix the garage; we'll fix the car. I just want to make sure you are all right."

Sure enough, when my Dad came home and saw the garage wall ripped from the ground, I just knew that he was going to come in the house and that this was going to be my last day on planet Earth. Instead, my Dad walked in and called me by my name as he came up the stairs. By now I was trembling. I had been afraid all day. I heard my Dad's voice; my sister was snickering in the corner, giggling as though it were funny.

Dad called my name. He hit the top of the stairs, and I stared him dead in the face. "Come here," he said. I walked very slowly. He leaned over and hugged me, and held me a long time. Then he said, "I love you more than I love that car and more than I love that garage. Next time, wait for me or your Mom to go with you." Talk about life coming back into my body; that was really close!

Having parents who will define your crashes and value you more than the damage caused by a crash is pivotal in a girl's life. Both of my parents, my Mom earlier that day and my Dad later that evening, affirmed me and valued my experience rather than the objects that were damaged.

When your daughter's adventurous nature takes her beyond the boundaries, make sure that you value her and affirm her. Do that no matter what she has found herself involved in, whether it is a relationship or a habit or the very thing that you have been anxious about (because you know your child). Never let the damage outweigh the value of your daughter. She's what's important—and she needs to know that!

Even in early crashes, salvage your child.

As I grew older, not long after the garage car crash, I jumped ahead of my season again.

My first marriage was at sixteen, when the Vietnam War was going on. I was in love with a very nice boy, and we got married to keep him from being drafted. That was in 1970. They were putting boys' names in the paper, and his name appeared for the draft. We were terrified. He was eighteen and a senior in high school, and they were drafting every male eighteen and above. Every day, the list of names was in the paper, and the individuals listed had thirty days to show up.

He was a year older than I was and he was scheduled to graduate in June. When his name appeared in the paper, his family went berserk. He was the youngest child of five. Everybody panicked. We were boyfriend and girlfriend, and although we were not in the same school, we were in the same choir. To resolve the family dilemma, his older brother told him, "Maybe you should get married, and then you won't have to go."

We had heard the story that if you got married, you wouldn't have to go, because you were then considered a head of household. We got the idea that we would get married, but still live separately with our parents, so that he could truthfully say he was married. And afterward, when he got out of school, we would live together. But we found out life doesn't work like that. The best of plans made too early, and without adults as resources, will always backfire.

As an unmarried man, my boyfriend would have had to report to the induction office in September for active duty, while I would be returning to school for my senior year. So our families had a meeting to discuss the plan we had made for him to avoid the draft.

It was a very uncomfortable meeting. My Mother had a fit, while my Father just sat quietly, very quietly. My boyfriend's Father was very quiet as well. It was a terrible meeting and I hated it. I knew I didn't want to get married. But I also didn't want my boyfriend to be killed in Vietnam. I had no idea that we were really going to consummate a marriage and live as husband and wife; that was the farthest thing from my mind. I was trying to get in the band, and I planned to graduate and then go on to college for nursing. Becoming a wife right now, with all the cooking, cleaning and responsibility that would entail, definitely wasn't part of that plan.

But to save my boyfriend from the draft and keep him from getting killed, I was willing to take off early in my "little chopper plane" that was still not completed, much less ready for a long and bumpy flight.

We convinced our parents to let us get married. My Mother had to sign for me, because I was still underage. Yet despite her resistance, she planned a beautiful wedding for me. I remember my Father walking me down the aisle of a jam-packed church. I was sixteen-years-old and my soon-to-be-husband was only eighteen. But I was a beautiful bride, and we went all out for the ceremony, with bridesmaids, beautiful decorations, and everything else that makes a wedding day special.

As my Daddy walked me down the aisle, he whispered, "You know, you don't have to do this."

I responded, "Daddy, the church is full!"

Then he said, in his deliberate cadence, "I can walk you in, or I can walk you out."

My Father was like that. He didn't talk a lot, but when he did talk, he was absolutely intentional and serious. He even slowed the walk down. "Oh, Daddy, no, don't do this," I cried.

"I'll turn you right around and walk you right out of here," he said. "You don't have to do this."

We did it anyway.

Prior to the wedding, my husband had been classified 1-A, and he was supposed to report for duty. But when we arrived downtown for him to report, the army had changed his status from 1-A to 4-F because he stuttered and had a hernia. He also did not do well on the entrance exam. So after all the concern and apprehension, he would no longer be going—not because we were married, but because his enlistment status had changed. But we were married. If only we had waited; if only I had listened to my Dad while we were walking down that aisle.

I should have listened. All along, my Father was looking out for me, trying to pull me back but still letting me have my freedom. But I crashed, and I crashed hard! Daddy saw the crash coming and so did my Mother. After my husband and I were divorced, ten years later, I asked my Father what it was that helped him keep his silence as he watched me prematurely take my maiden flight and lose altitude, clipping trees and wires on my way down. He said his responsibility was to watch and be prepared to rescue me whenever I realized that I needed to evacuate my broken aircraft.

I remember the pre-wedding meeting, when Dad didn't say anything. I remember that neither he nor my boyfriend's Father said anything. Men see things very differently; I've learned that. Men are very different from women in what they think is a priority and what is not, and how they address it.

My Father's silence was very powerful in that meeting, *very powerful*. I knew he didn't like my plan to fly early, and I knew I was going hear something from him about it. However, even with his displeasure about my decision, he helped me through that entire experience.

Most of our ill-fated marriage was filled with yelling and fighting, distrust, and jealousy, along with immaturity about resolving conflicts. We had two beautiful, gifted daughters. I was finishing nursing school, and hubby was unemployed, trying to get a job. At that point, his Mother was telling him he had to have a job, now that he had a wife and children. Much later, he was able to secure training and a career, but our plane had already begun its descent.

Thank God for my Father! He was there for me even after I crashed. He was doing triage in the midst of the crash, and he was supportive long afterward. See, your daughter needs you when she crashes even more than when she soars!

When in crisis, daughters without Dads tend to have limited ability to deal with their own trauma, poor choices and mistakes. In the midst of the crash, your daughter needs to know from you, Dad, what is happening, why, and how to keep it from happening again. She needs your guidance to ensure that her next flights will be successful and on time, not departing early from the runway, and in the right vehicle for maximum altitude.

Daughters (and sons) who lack Dads can carry emotional baggage that is far too heavy for the maximum weight of their aircraft. That baggage can ultimately cause them to veer from the flight plans intended for their lives. The weight these women carry devastates both them and their children, and it also skews their view of future opportunities later in life.

Your goal, Dad, is to help your daughter get out of the crash safely and back into training so that when it's time for her to fly again, she will be mentally and emotionally ready, and equipped to go to the highest altitude available. Even though she will sometimes encounter turbulence from her early crash experience, she will now be better prepared to make the necessary adjustments for landing safely, with all of her passengers in tow.

Dad, you are the primary air traffic controller for your daughter's flight plans. You and Mom are integral participants who monitor the radars for safe takeoffs and landings. Communications and tracking are both essential for this role. The radios must be working on both ends. Initiation and feedback must be regularly engaged, both on and off the ground. You cannot wait until a catastrophe happens to begin communicating with your daughter. In an ideal situation, you and Mom are the two voices that she will always recognize.

Air traffic controllers are well-organized, have assertive and firm decision-making ability, and are able to maintain their cool and composure under pressure. Dad, you must have excellent hearing and speaking skills, long-term perception, and discernment. Teach your daughter exact words and their meanings. In a crisis, she will need to know what the instructions mean at that moment and not have to choose from several options. She should know exactly what you mean when you say what you say.

The most important thing to know is that your daughter's adventures don't have to leave her with permanent scars. She must fly again, but she *needs* you. Without you, her injuries can be fatal. With you, she doesn't have to crash at all. If she does crash, you're there to pick her up, hug her, affirm her, and equip her for future successful flights.

My Daddy did it, and Dad, you can, too.

TAKEAWAYS

- What are you doing now to help ensure that your daughter can make good decisions?
- Has your daughter crashed? What can you do to make sure she will recover?
- Is your daughter about to crash? What does your wisdom and foresight tell you to do to help her avoid crashing?

CHAPTER 7

●●●

Daughter's Daddy Issues

"I can't find my way without you, Dad."

What is the impact on a daughter who has no Father in her life, either through divorce, death or emotional absence? Is it possible for this girl to grow into a healthy, stable woman in her adult years after not having a close relationship with her Father? Does this one fact make a huge difference in her achievements, relationships and self-esteem?

In *Fly Away Home*, young Amy was critical of her Father at the beginning. She resented the fact that her Father had previously chosen to live his life without her. She was unimpressed with his home and housekeeping, his occupation, his way of life and his living arrangements. She mocked his hobby of constructing solo-occupant aircraft, and was visibly alarmed that he would take risks with his little flying contraption.

Divorce, abandonment and death are the primary causes of a daughter not knowing her Dad, but a more insidious form of absenteeism can take place with the Dad being right in the home. Fathers can *neglect* their parental role without ever leaving the home. These are Fathers who are in the home but are not "there for their daughters." They're present physically but they're not *really* present. They're emotionally and spiritually absent. They live in the home, but they do not take on their Fatherly role.

The absent Father isn't just a man who's not present. The man who does not interact with his daughter on a regular basis and, therefore, does not play a significant role in her development, is also absent. He may live at home, but he neglects to nurture the child nonetheless.

Fathers who live in the home with their daughters but do not play active roles in their daughters' development cause these young women to second-guess their own actions. Meanwhile, such Dads force the daughters' Mothers to act as both parents, consequently putting a strain on the Mother-daughter relationship. And as the daughter grows into a woman, she's going to suffer from Father-Hunger, causing her to resent the dominant parent.

Often these Father-Hunger issues, or Daddy issues, don't reveal themselves until a girl has become a young adult. In my experience as a pastoral counselor, one gleaming and repetitive observation that I have made is that these women struggle with love and approval. These girls often feel unsupported and unattractive. Even if the Father was a good provider, the girl still needs her Dad's emotional attention. This is how her self-worth and self-esteem blossom. When she hears her Dad say, "You are so pretty," or, "That is a lovely dress," or, "I really like your hair," he sets a precedence of affirming statements that build her self-worth more than any gift, trinket or reward. Oftentimes, however, a woman who has grown up with an emotionally absent Father ends up in relationships with men just like him.

"Daddy issues" is a broad and vague term that covers just about all manifestations of Father-Hunger. Whether Dad was physically absent or physically present but emotionally unavailable—or physically, emotionally or sexually abusive—the patterns that evolve constitute "Daddy issues."

I once read a powerful article that talked about "paternal estrangement." I learned that parental estrangement is as the heart of a child's "Daddy issues." Here's a truth: Daughters still need their natural Fathers, even when a Stepfather is trying to step in.

When a daughter is estranged from her Father, she develops unhealthy patterns.

These include being attracted only to older men, whose stability and confidence are attractive to a woman who lacked security in childhood. An older man may become a surrogate Father by providing the affection she lacked in her youth.

Jealousy and clinginess are other signs of Daddy issues. Insecurity causes such women to worry that their partners will leave them. Such insecurity breeds paranoia, which manifests in behaviors such as checking a boyfriend's cellphone for hints of infidelity or even following him around. Women with Daddy issues need to be constantly reminded that they're adored. They compare themselves to other women.

Some women with Daddy issues also have issues with sex. They feel loved when they're having sex, so they sometimes engage in risky sexual behaviors. Such women appear to base their own worth on their perceived sexual desirability. Unfortunately, sex in itself is not love. Women who use sex as a love offering rarely get to know real sexual intimacy, which is based on true love, mutual respect and companionship.

Some women with Daddy issues are fearful of being alone. They'd rather be in a dysfunctional relationship than be single. They're unable to develop their own unique identities without a lot of intentional work. They also have trouble with correction and discipline.

"Every time you talk to me, it cuts me, it just cuts me." I have heard this statement hundreds of times when speaking to young women who have no Father's voice in their ear.

I reply, "Honey, I would never try to hurt you. Why would I?" This is a difficult moment to assess if you don't know this one important detail—Father-Hunger—about the girl you are addressing. She appears whole and healthy, but until you prick this area and see her reaction, you will never know how well she has covered up her hurt.

I asked myself many times, "Why do these women say I'm cutting them with what I say? Why do they always get so sensitive or offended?"

Answer: They have never had a Father. So when I speak to them in a tone of parental authority, they don't know what that is supposed to sound like, or what it means.

I've learned to explain to young women that I'm not speaking to them as a woman; I'm speaking to them in the voice of a Father. When I'm in a confrontational type of meeting with a woman who hasn't known a Father's authority, I say, "I need you to hear my voice as a Father's voice." I explain that this is what a Father would do. This is how a Father would say it.

Too many women don't know that. That's why they're so fragile. They don't know the sound of the Father's voice. And since they don't know that voice, they also don't know its authority or affirmation. When they hear the sound of such a voice now, as from me, they feel small and unloved. They feel anger and sometimes shame. Anger and shame are defense mechanisms against anything that makes them feel ignorant and unlearned. So they need to appear smart about everything.

Such a woman is uncomfortable with anything she is not excelling in. Oftentimes, it's not because she isn't smart, but because she has never allowed anyone to teach her what she doesn't know. And she never wants you to know what she doesn't know.

An entire generation of women has its shield up: "Don't mess with me." But if these women had known their Fathers' love, it might be different. It *would* be different. Because a Father sets boundaries while making you feel good about yourself. Boundaries are not punitive; boundaries are for your protection. Fathers set the laws. Fathers make you safe. Fathers make you pretty and important.

Many Dads who have daughters in the house are afraid to touch them. They are afraid to give the physically demonstrative (but non-sexual) love their daughters need because they don't know how. I can go back to the fact that these men probably didn't know the loving touch of their own Fathers, either. A Father teaches you how to touch, how to hug, how to love safely.

This is of absolute importance. Fathers aren't doing this today because *their* Fathers didn't do it. A generation of men—in fact, maybe two or three generations of men—has thought it wrong to hug their sons, to say, "I love you." They were wrong. And these generations of men have also been standoffish with their daughters, because they didn't know how to approach the "task" of showing loving affection to a daughter who is maturing into a woman.

Father-Hunger causes trouble in educational settings and with the law; it's a cause of poverty, substance abuse, and health issues—both physical and mental.

We also have to look at some of the more perverse results of Father-Hunger. Impurity among men and women, which goes against God's original intent, has released great perversions into the world. They include rape, same-gender sexual relationships, and molestation. Sometimes, the Father is the molester, and much of that perversion is rooted in a misunderstanding of sex and love.

I believe many men only know how to touch women one way: sexually. Men associate deep emotional attraction for a woman with sex. That's because men are psychologically unprepared to deal with their own emotions. And sometimes they confuse other emotions with paternal love for a child. In other words, a man whose own orientation has been distorted can be sexually attracted to his own daughters.

The incest relationship usually starts very "innocently." Daughters look up to their Fathers. They have a deep trust and respect for the man who gives them a sense of security. When a husband and wife are having marital difficulties, the husband sometimes turns to the daughter to meet the needs that the wife should fulfill.

The incestuous relationship may go on for years, resulting in long-term, emotional damage to the daughter. She is likely to have issues about trust, cleanliness (often these women have phobias about dirt), loud noises, and being alone in the dark. She probably has trust issues with men in general and finds it difficult to remain committed in a relationship with a man. She may be promiscuous, yet never marry. Or if she does marry, the same girl can become frigid.

Father-daughter incest is a horrible type of betrayal; it is extremely devastating to the daughter, and can be seen as the worse form of betrayal that can happen to a girl. Psychologist Diana Russell calls Father-daughter incest the *"supreme betrayal."*[25]

Various studies show that female survivors of incest tend to experience severe rage, hostility and contempt toward their parents and toward men in general. They are less likely to marry than other women, and those who do marry have great difficulty with emotional and sexual intimacy. Trust is also a major issue for them, and many of these survivors become victims of domestic violence.

Survivors can also struggle with learning difficulties and short attention spans, low-to-no self-esteem, nightmares, insomnia, stomach ailments, and migraines.

A man who commits incest with a daughter exposes his own impurity, since he knows only *erotic* love. He is incapable of the non-erotic, healthy paternal love of a Father for a daughter. Therefore, his daughter becomes his victim, since he is inappropriately aroused sexually by her presence. *The love a Father has for his daughter should never be erotic.*

INCEST

I want to bring this out into the open. I want to discuss what happens when Fathers commit sexual acts with their own daughters. Now, don't think it doesn't happen in your community. Today, some Fathers rape their own daughters, molest their own children, and even sire offspring through their daughters.

What does that do to a girl? I've seen it so much. I counsel a woman who had children by her own Father. She later had a relationship with the pastor of a church she attended and now has a child by him as well. Her Father forced a pattern on her.

As another example, I counseled a couple in which both the husband and the wife had been in and out of several prior marriages. I got alone with the young lady, who was so broken and so hurt that I was being very tender with her.

"How was your relationship with your Father?" I asked. She just started bawling. Her Dad had molested her, so her perception and orientation toward commitment were skewed. Now working on her third marriage, she was very discontented and unhappy. She felt unfulfilled and blamed herself for not being loved.

This woman was so broken, yet with different variations, I have heard this same story told hundreds of times in my office. The victim and villain syndrome is rampant among women who have had incestuous relationships. They take love very seriously, and want it desperately, so they look in all the wrong places, and when they don't get what they need, they vilify themselves until they find another partner to try out. This pattern often leads to multiple marriages and, sadly, divorces.

Men, while I'm against it, there's enough free booty in the world; you don't ever have to molest your child. People will give you sex for no charge.

When I think about all the girls out there who are being molested by their Fathers and Stepfathers and uncles—men who are supposed to protect them—I get really angry. Incest is the ultimate in impropriety and betrayal. Yes, rape by a stranger is devastating. But rape by her protector can destroy a woman's soul. How does any woman delete rape from her memory? How painful and deeply embedded in her psyche is it when she doesn't know the predator? Now, think for a moment. How much more painful do you think it is when a girl knew and trusted the villain, and now must live with that memory forever?

Dad, let me speak to you as your daughter. If you're intending to protect me and provide security for me, then I'm already vulnerable to you. I'm already open to you. There are no barriers between us. Why would you take that as sexual attraction?

The emotional baggage these betrayed daughters carry makes my gut wrench. I hear their hurt, I hear their pain, and I hear what it did to them when their Fathers not only failed to protect their vulnerability and purity but instead took advantage of their innocence.

Such travesties cause girls to be angry with their Mothers, especially when they believe their Mothers didn't defend them. Therefore, contention and strife with their Mothers is part of the emotional baggage these daughters carry.

Now, the Mother may have known or she may not have known. She may have buried her head in the sand to deny that her husband molested his own daughter. But a Mother who knows something is sexually wrong between her husband and his daughter creates extreme resentment with her silence.

In past eras, Mothers were more likely to go silent. Me, I would have gone ballistic. My own Mother might not have gone ballistic, since her generation didn't act like my generation. Nine times out of ten, a woman of her generation would have dealt with this sort of thing internally. The daughter then had no parent to turn to, so a destructive life pattern was established.

Remember, I am talking about incest. So what happens to a daughter whose Father was her predator?

Soon the girl's lying in bed with another man; she's pregnant with her first child or possibly her second. She's not married. She moves from one man to another, looking for the same attention she received from her Father. The men are sexually interesting, but not in any valid way because her sexual orientation is off. She doesn't connect sexual activity to marriage or to love; she connects it to validating herself through this person who is having sex with her. She learned from her Father than sex is not necessarily for pleasure. His message was, "You won't like this. But this is what you do if you love me."

SAME-SEX LOVE

Lesbianism may be the result of multiple factors in the home, one of which is Father-Hunger; another is Mother-daughter tension; and sometimes there is also physical or emotional abuse. A young woman will seek protection, and if another woman is willing to provide that, offers financial support, or fills any other Father roles, then she will find the love she needs in the arms of this other woman.

Many women discover their attraction to another woman after several failed relationships or marriages with men. Or they may be discontented with the lack of emotional support men provide.

A woman is most likely to pursue a relationship with another woman when it begins on an emotional level. After the attachment is deep enough, it leads to sexual activity. The intensity of the emotional bond and responses is far more important than the physical pleasure of sex alone. This is the aspect that is often misunderstood in heterosexual relationships; the way a man responds to a woman's emotional needs has the potential to either validate her or deeply injure her. If the male only responds sexually, the woman may not be fulfilled in that relationship. After many failed attempts with men, a woman may choose to entrust her heart to another female.

Other instances of lesbian love stem from resentment and anger issues with Mother. A daughter who is angry and resentful toward her Mother may take on very masculine traits. She seeks control and dominance because she never wants to be seen as the weak, unresponsive woman she perceives her Mother to be.

That perception may have arisen in the home when the Mother was silent about incest. Or the Mother may have abandoned the daughter because of work, or because she lost custody or got a divorce. Not every woman turns to same sex love for these reasons, but these are some of the variables we should consider.

Anne Paulk has a great deal of experience in this area of life. As an author, past Exodus International board member, and former lesbian, she conducted a 2001 study directed at women who were attempting to overcome homosexuality. 265 women responded, with the results showing many preconditioning factors:

- 69.1 percent had experienced emotional abuse.

- 55.7 percent had experienced emotional trauma, including trauma resulting from sexual innuendoes and specific sexual remarks that made them feel violated.
- 66.4 percent had been victims of sexual abuse.
- 53.2 percent had been verbally abused.
- 39.6 percent felt abandoned.
  32.5 percent had been victims of physical abuse.
- 20.0 percent felt "utterly neglected."

Males were responsible for almost 80 percent of the sexual abuse reported by the respondents. Forty-two percent of the sexual abuse took place in the context of incestuous relationships and 20 percent involved molestation by females.[26]

Lesbianism is never just sexually motivated or driven; for girls, the greater need is consistent, affirming, loving concern. In my experience as a counselor and life coach, I have come to the conclusion *that the lesbian struggle is an identity crisis, not a sexual orientation problem.* Girls need their Dads to affirm who they are and to do it well. Affirming, loving concern should come first from the Father and then from the Mother, so that no daughter is left wanting or needing in this aspect of her development. My experience as an educator in multiple female environments shows that lesbians are searching for a basic sense of self, as well as for an identity, and that their concept of femininity has been distorted.

FACTS AND DATA

- Countless supporting facts and data show that Fatherless daughters suffer deficits in many areas of their development.

In one major study, the authors state, "The ways in which [females lacking Fathers] view the opposite sex, the outside world and themselves are forever tainted as a result of missing the key element of a Father."[27]

The San Francisco Bay Area Male Involvement Network's newsletter, *Getting Men Involved*, notes the following statistics:

* 63% of youth suicides are from Fatherless homes.

* 90% of all homeless, runaway children are from Fatherless homes.

* 85% of all children who exhibit behavioral disorders come from Fatherless homes.

* 80% of rapists motivated by displaced anger come from Fatherless homes.

* 71% of all high school dropouts are from Fatherless homes.

* 75% of all adolescent patients in chemical abuse centers come from Fatherless homes.

* 70% of juveniles in state-oriented institutions come from Fatherless homes.

* 85% of all youths in prisons grew up in Fatherless homes.[28]

The National Center for Fathering (NCF) notes: "Almost every social ill faced by America's children is related to Fatherlessness."[29] The NCF also lists six major areas of concern:

- **Poverty.** "Children in Father-absent homes are almost four times more likely to be poor."[30] According to U.S. Census Bureau statistics, in 2011, 12 percent of children in married-couple families were living in poverty, compared to 44 percent of children in Mother-only families. U.S. Department of Health and Human Services statistics are similar: "Children living in female-headed families with no spouse present had a poverty rate of 47.6 percent, over four times the rate of married-couple families."[31]

- **Substance abuse.** The U.S. Department of Health and Human Services states: "Fatherless children are at a dramatically greater risk of drug and alcohol abuse.'"[32] The NCF states: "There is significantly more drug use among children who do not live with their Mother and Father," citing an article by John P. Hoffman in *The Journal of Marriage and Family* titled "The Community Context of Family Structure and Adolescent Drug Use."[33] And an NCF web link formerly cited an article in *The International Journal of the Addictions* that asserted: "Children who live apart from their Fathers are 4.3 times more likely to smoke cigarettes as teenagers than children growing up with Fathers in the home."[34]

- **Crime**. Citing the *Journal of Research in Crime and Delinquency,* the NCF stated: "Adolescents living in intact families are less likely to engage in delinquency than their peers living in non-intact families. Compared to peers in intact families, adolescents in single-parent families and stepfamilies were more likely to engage in delinquency. This relationship appeared to be operating through differences in family processes—parental involvement, supervision, monitoring, and parent-child closeness—between intact and non-intact families."[35]

- **Behavioral problems and physical ailments**. "A study of 1,977 children, age three and older and living with a residential Father or Father figure, found that children living with married biological parents had significantly fewer externalizing and internalizing behavioral problems than children living with at least one non-biological parent."[36] "Children of single-parent homes are more than twice as likely to commit suicide."[37] "Three out of four teenage suicides occur in households where a parent has been absent."[38] "Children born to single Mothers show higher levels of aggressive behavior than children born to married Mothers. Living in a single-Mother household is equivalent to experiencing 5.25 partnership transitions."[39]

- **Educational deficits**. Studies show that children without cohabiting parents have lower grade point averages, less regular school attendance and higher dropout rates. Fewer Fatherless children go to college. "Children living with their married, biological Father tested at a significantly higher level than those living with a non-biological Father"[40] Citing a paper from the U.S. Department of Education's National Center for Education Statistics, the NCF said a Father's active involvement in his child's school increases the likelihood of a student getting good grades. "This was true for Fathers in biological parent families, for Stepfathers, and for Fathers heading single-parent families."[41]

- **Sexual deficits**. The NCF reported that 71 percent of high school dropouts are Fatherless.[42] When it comes to sexual activity and teen pregnancy, adolescent females age fifteen to nineteen are more likely to engage in premarital sexual activity if they live in homes without Fathers.[43]

CRIME

An article in the *Social Psychology Quarterly* notes that a study using a national probability sample of 1,636 young men and women found that teenage males and females alike, from female-headed households, are more likely to commit criminal acts than those whose Fathers are present. Other studies bear out that males are more likely to commit crimes, while females are more likely to have Fatherless children.[44]

Criminal activity on the part of children without Fathers is only one facet of the Fatherlessness-and-crime problem.

The NCF points to another article to emphasize that Fatherless kids are also more likely to be victimized by crime:

> *Children age ten to seventeen living with two biological or adoptive parents were significantly less likely to experience sexual assault, child maltreatment, other types of major violence, and non-victimization types of adversity, and were less likely to witness violence in their families compared to peers living in single-parent families and stepfamilies.*[45]

Citing another article, the NCF says that neighborhoods with a high percentage of Father-less families have a higher incidence of teen-on-teen violence.

> *If the number of Fathers is low in a neighborhood, then there is an increase in acts of teen violence. The statistical data showed that a 1 percent increase in the proportion of single-parent families in a neighborhood is associated with a 3 percent increase in an adolescent's level of violence. In other words, adolescents who live in neighborhoods with lower proportions of single-parent families and who report higher levels of family integration commit less violence.*[46]

MENTAL HEALTH

Each year in the United States, children's mental health issues continue to escalate. Cost estimates as high as $247 billion are quoted to bring attention to these needs. One major center notes: "A study of nearly 6,000 children found that children from single-parent homes had more physical and mental health problems than children who lived with two married parents."[47] Moreover, "Girls with absent Fathers grow up without the day-by-day experience of attentive, caring and loving interaction with a man. Without this continuous sense of being valued and loved, a young girl does not thrive but rather is stunted in her emotional development."[48]

The coping mechanisms of adolescent girls whose Fathers are absent after divorce include:

- Intensified separation anxiety.
- Denial and avoidance of feelings associated with the loss of a Father.
- Identification with the lost object.
- Object hunger for males.[49]

Finally, I offer you this quote: "The negative effects later in life have been well documented, with numerous studies indicating that girls from Fatherless families develop more promiscuous attitudes and experience difficulty in forming or maintaining romantic relations later in their development."[50] These behavioral patterns are carried with them into womanhood and may be the cause of their unfulfilling relationships with men.

SEXUAL ACTIVITY

Dad, did you know that your presence—or lack thereof—has a direct effect on your daughter's sexuality? Consider the following:

- A study using a sample of 1409 rural, southern adolescents (851 females and 558 males) age eleven to eighteen years, investigated the correlation between Father absence and self-reported sexual activity. The results revealed that adolescents in Father-absent homes were more likely to report being sexually active compared to adolescents living with their Fathers.[51]

- Being raised by a single Mother raises the risk of teen pregnancy, marrying with less than a high school degree, and forming a marriage where both partners have less than a high school degree.[52]

It should be noted "that for females to have inconstant relationships with their Fathers can have a devastating effect ... by making them more vulnerable to outside influences that lead them into impure relationships and childbearing before they're ready.[53] Such women are:

- 53% more likely to marry as teenagers.
- 111% more likely to have children as teenagers.
- 164% more likely to be a single parent.
- 92% more likely to divorce if they marry.[54]

EDUCATION

I don't know of any father who doesn't want his daughter to obtain the best education possible. However: "Fatherless children have more trouble academically, scoring poorly on tests of reading, mathematics, and thinking skills; children from Father-absent homes are more likely to be truant from school, more likely to be excluded from school, more likely to leave school at age sixteen, and less likely to attain academic and professional qualifications in adulthood."[55]

According to the landmark book, *Where's Daddy? How Divorced, Single, and Widowed Women Can Provide What's Missing When Dad's Missing* by Claudette Wassil-Grimm, females who lack Father figures are more prone to experience diminished cognitive development, affecting how they perform on achievement tests and IQ tests.[56]

Another study showed that Fathers play "significant" roles in female achievement in mathematics.[57]

Mathematics is typically associated with masculinity; therefore, females without Father figures may have less interest in this subject matter. Female high school seniors were more likely than their male peers to say they did not take mathematics and science. ... Essentially, females are discouraged from pursuing a career in mathematics, and Father absence contributes to this phenomenon by not providing them with a male role model to stimulate their interest in this area.[58]

Gender bias may play a role. Lack of attention given to girls by teachers in the classroom appears to be real, and different expectations for girls affect their performance in math and science. Various studies show that classroom teachers not only call on boys more often than girls, but listen more when boys call out answers. Since teachers assume that girls will be conscientious students, they tend to encourage boys more often by commenting on their work, offering suggestions, and giving praise.[59]

These facts greatly affect female achievement in mathematics and other academic areas, since girls are less likely to be given adequate attention or taught to attempt that which is foreign to them. Females are restricted to societal expectations of them and are rarely asked to go outside this frame.[60]

I'd like to offer various quotes from the authors of another major study, *"The Effects Absent Fathers Have on Female Development and College Attendance."* The authors explain that the formative years of a girl's life are crucial not just to her education but to her ability to learn. They also state:

> *A number of more recent, controlled studies are generally consistent with the supposition that Father-absent children, at least those from lower-class backgrounds, are less likely to function well in intelligence and aptitude tests than are Father-present children. This phenomenon typically occurs as a result of the Mother having to act as both breadwinner and homemaker. The duplicate role the Mother plays limits the children from receiving the type of attention they need and deserve.*

> *Early, long term, and complete Father absence was especially likely to be related negatively to intellectual competence.*

> *The family instability and financial difficulty often associated with divorce and Father Absence may be primary factors interfering with the child's cognitive functioning. However, the major disadvantage related*

to Father Absence for children is lessened paternal attention, including fewer opportunities to model mature decision-making and problem solving.

The decrease in Father involvement typically associated with divorce can contribute to potentially serious problems in various development areas of a school-aged child's functioning, including academic and cognitive defects as well as social adjustment and peer relationship handicaps and mental and physical health difficulties. Problems for school-aged children have been found to be generally more severe for boys and girls growing up in lower socioeconomic circumstances, but even children from affluent families are at risk. Low socioeconomic status may be an additional stressor, but it by no means transcends the risk of inadequate Father Involvement.[61]

The same study also explains why some women struggle in college, noting: "Total Father-absence before age ten was highly associated with a deficit in quantitative aptitude. In addition, Father-absence during the age period from three to seven may have especially negative effects on academic aptitude."[62]

The study goes on to say: "College is harder to afford for children of single parents. For women particularly, entering the workforce is a more viable opportunity to have a sense of financial security. This phenomenon of female liberation through a paycheck is very disturbing since it limits Fatherless daughters from achieving higher education and creates the falsehood that a paycheck can act as healing.

Expecting to find freedom in pay is very detrimental because it does not allow Fatherless females to deal with their true feelings about their Fathers' absence.'"[63]

WHEN AND WHY DADDY LEAVES MAKES A DIFFERENCE.

HOW Father departed and WHEN he departed are factors that affect a female's educational development. The age of the child when Daddy left and the circumstances of his departure both affect the child's development, including her cognitive development and her educational achievement. Consider the following: "Divorce, death, and abandonment are all forms of absence [that] affect female development differently. The age at which a daughter loses her Father is meaningful since it influences her perceptions of males and the world as well as her academic advancement."[64]

There are also significant differences between girls whose Fathers died and those whose Fathers were not present for other reasons.

- The most detrimental effects occurred when Father-absence was due to divorce, desertion, or separation, rather than to death. Father-absent daughters via death understand that their Father did not abandon them and learn to excuse his absence as a result of his passing. Consequently, they do not possess hatred toward their Fathers.

- Girls who had little contact with their Fathers, especially during adolescence, had great difficulties forming lasting relationships with men. Sadly, these females either shy away from males altogether or become sexually aggressive. Girls with involved

Fathers learn how to interact with males by using the Father-daughter relationship as a model. They not only have a concerned male to converse with but also have a feeling of acceptance, knowing they are loved by at least one male. Females without Father figures often become desperate for male attention.[65]

On many occasions, I have recognized this particular characteristic in very isolated and private women. In each such case, it usually comes from losing the Father very early in life, sometimes even in infancy. The girl never had a chance to relate to her Dad and she now becomes very protective of her own children. If she has indeed married and has a family, this woman will assume the roles of both Father and Mother, filling the role of Father in the way she wishes her Father had done for her.

Daughters whose Fathers died early suffer from deep Father-Hunger very differently than girls caught in the midst of divorce or abandonment. Consider the following information:

- Females deprived of a Father as a result of his death tend to have the most positive concept of the Father while feeling the saddest about his disappearance. Girls whose Fathers died before they reached the age of five are extremely reticent around male adults; they shy away from physical contact with them and rarely smile. Furthermore, daughters of widows are less likely to have a lot of anger toward males, or toward adults in general, and are also unlikely to seek immense amounts of attention from them. In terms of sexuality, daughters of widows are likely to be afraid of men, while daughters of divorced parents tend to be "clumsily erotic."

- Females who lose their Fathers through divorce or abandonment seek much more attention from men and have more physical contact with boys their age than do girls from intact homes. They also tend to be more critical of their Fathers and the opposite sex. These females constantly seek replacements for their missing Fathers. As a result, they have a constant need to be accepted by the men from whom they aggressively seek attention.[66]

Studies done in the 1990s that compared daughters of widows, divorcees and intact families obtained similar results. Daughters of divorce seek much more attention from men and boys their age, and they are critical of their Fathers. They exhibit more aggressive behavior and constantly seek attention from adults, and they are physically aggressive toward both male and female peers. Meanwhile, daughters of widows are more likely to avoid contact with males and to have positive concepts of their Fathers. They also feel sadder about losing their Fathers than the daughters of divorced parents do.[67]

Why would I quote all this information? To bore you? To fill up pages in my book? No. I understand that Dads are logical. They need to hear "just the facts." So I've given you lots of facts and data so that you will know I'm not just stating my own opinions here.

Dad, for your daughter's sake, BE PRESENT, BE HEALTHY, BE ENGAGED and BE COMMITTED to her well-being and success. Let nothing short of death stop you from loving her and living a balanced and rounded life before her. Get the help you need to support her and *never give up on your relationship with her.*

TAKEAWAYS

- Do you see yourself in any of the quoted material? If so, can you now understand the effect you have on your daughter?
- Of all the facts and data quoted, what has impacted you the most?
- Can you ask your daughter to forgive you for not being as present in her life as you've wanted to be and she has needed you to be?

CHAPTER 8

●●●

Phenomenal Fathering

"I'm involved too, Amy, these are not just your geese!"

When Amy Alden took responsibility for her clutch of eggs, Thomas Alden became responsible for them, too. He was not hands-on with the geese; he let her do the nurturing. But the geese were his daughter's, and she was his daughter, so the geese also became part of his charge. Rather than working through the day-to-day care of the geese, he saw the much bigger picture. Here is what he needed to do with Amy for the geese. He had to:

- Protect.
- Provide.
- Define.
- Set boundaries.
- Establish order.
- Discipline and correct.
- Be present.
- Affirm.
- Love.
- Sacrifice.

As soon as Alden became aware that the geese were in peril if they stayed too long at his farm, he began the work of protecting them. He was not as overtly concerned about the geese as Amy was; he was acting on the geese's behalf for the sole purpose of protecting his still-fragile daughter in the aftermath of losing her Mother and being totally displaced from her comfort zone. He was striving to be a phenomenal Father.

To be a phenomenal Father, you must first start with some basics of nurturing, and with love and concern for successful outcomes. Foundationally, a Father is responsible for the physical, mental, social, emotional, and spiritual needs of a child. Men, you must understand: As a Father, you are irreplaceable. Your daughter needs your security and stability; she also needs provision. She needs love. Your daughter needs your acceptance. Your daughter needs discipline. She needs self-control. She will need independence and recognition of her worth, and you, Dad, are the source to provide all these things.

PROTECT AND PROVIDE

Your daughter needs security as her foundation from birth, continuing through her childhood and adolescence into early adulthood. The stability that comes from a secure home base with an active Father diminishes childhood anxiety; it allows the children to be children, to focus their minds on discovery rather than insecurity.

Your daughter's security and stability come from your role as protector and provider. As the head of the household, as the Father, you're responsible for ensuring that your daughter will grow up with all of her needs covered to the best of your ability, including a safe home with electricity and heat, food, and clothing. Because your love is ever giving and perceptive, you must see to those needs first.

In addition, as your daughter's protector, you provide guidelines and rules. You establish boundaries, which will change as your daughter grows. As her protector, you're there to monitor her. You will keep bad influences out and teach her the positives. You'll have to modify your approach as your daughter grows, but you'll always be "on watch" and ready to act as she explores her world. You'll also have to interpret the world around her *for* her, because she can't see the motives of others as well as a Father can.

My Father protected my sisters and me from bad influences throughout our childhood, in our neighborhood, on our block, and elsewhere. Daddy protected me from boys throughout my youth, and then he tried his best to protect me when I was old enough to make decisions on my own. He definitely could see better than I could the consequences of my own actions.

I remember several incidents in which my Dad could see the reality before anyone else did. For instance, one of my sisters became friends with a neighbor girl who had a few emotional issues and negative influences. This girl was feeding my sister the wrong kind of information, and she was also feeding my sister, literally. They would get together and eat and eat and eat, and my sister started gaining weight, emotionally and physically.

So my Father went over to my sister's friend's house one day; I never will forget it. He knocked on the door and said, "Is my daughter here?"

"Yes, she's here," somebody called back.

"Well, bring her out; bring her out, right now."

That's what a phenomenal Father will do.

On other occasions, when boys were hovering around our home because there were three pretty girls in it, Dad would totally embarrass those who showed interest in any of his girls. He would ask them the most pointed questions, as if they were on the witness stand in a courtroom.

"What's your name? Where do you live? What do your parents do for a living, and where do they work? Do you go to church? What do you want to be when you grow up?" Now, understand that these interrogations went on in full view of us girls. We would be so embarrassed that we would throw up our hands and holler, "Oh, forget it! Dad! Are you serious?" Then our Father would turn around and say to us, "Get inside the house, because if he cannot answer my questions, he cannot talk to my daughters." And he was serious.

A Father has to be careful about the people who come around his daughters—whether they are men, women, or children—because "birds of a feather flock together." For example, a flock of little girls who are reclusive could affirm themselves in that position. Then the Father has to take the daughter away from that situation and say, "No, that's not your reality."

I was always safe. If anyone tried to violate me in any way, my Father got rid of that person. And I never even knew when he/she was gone.

The Father is a protector. Fathers make you safe. So many women don't know that.

I got harder to handle in my teens, and my sweet, poor Daddy had to stay strong. Not only did he have to protect me from boys, he had to protect boys from me —or more precisely, protect me from myself and my own "I'm-all-grown-up" mentality.

When I was an adolescent, one of our church deacons' grandsons would visit every year. This boy was much older than I was and cute as a button, and every year we liked each other more. Now, my Dad was convinced that I was not going to date until I was out of high school. I wasn't supposed to have a phone call from a male until I was sixteen. These were well-known guidelines. Mother articulated them to me, but they weren't her rules. They were my Father's rules.

One summer when I was between thirteen and fourteen, a young man in particular was really after me. My gosh, he was really coming on strong. We concocted a plan that he would come by my house one night.

My Father had built a garage, and we were the only family around that had one, so I didn't know we were poor. In fact, I thought we were wealthy. Anyway, I came up with an idea. I told my young man, "My Dad's going to be home, but my Mom's going to be working a little part-time job at night, so I'm going to sneak out of the house and meet you behind the garage."

Now, I was a teenager and I was pretty stupid, because I thought Daddy would never know we were there. The garage was in back, off the alley, and I was very quiet about going down the stairs and opening the doors.

Well, the boy and I met as planned behind our garage. He was driving a gray Impala, which was the deacon's car, and he had brought me something to drink. I don't remember what it was, but I soon had a little buzz going from it. Then we started kissing, and the windows in the Impala started to fog up. He said, "Let's get into the back seat."

And we did. It was summer and very hot, and the windows were foggy. Then this paramour of mine said, "Why don't you take off your top?"

"No, no, no, I can't do that," I said.

"Why not? There's nobody here but us," he replied, using the same old line that men always use in these situations.

I was pretty naïve. Not only was I a virgin, but I was really pure. I didn't know much about anything then. In my youth, TV shows weren't full of sex, and there was no Internet then. There was nothing foul in my periphery, so I was just pure. Right then, I only knew that we were kissing up a storm and I was having a wonderful time. I felt like an adult and very mature. My baby sisters were in the house asleep, my Dad was asleep, and my Mom was at work. What could stop us, right?

Knock, knock, knock!

We both jumped, but didn't respond.

Within seconds came more knocks on the window, each one louder and more persistent. Knock, knock. Then, KNOCK, KNOCK, KNOCK.

We froze. Who could it be? We couldn't run, we couldn't hide, and we couldn't even see out the window. We didn't know who the heck it was.

Then I heard my Daddy. "Corletta, roll this window down."

At that moment, I wished I were invisible. What was Daddy doing outside, knocking on the window? How did he know where to come? Did he hear me leave the house?

It was so hot in that car that when I rolled the window down, steam came out.

Daddy said, "Come on. Get out. Get in the house."

I did as I was told. I don't know what Daddy told that boy, and I don't know what he told his Grandfather. But as far as I know, the poor guy never came back to Detroit again. My Father was protecting me from myself when I didn't even know I needed protecting. That's what phenomenal Fathers do.

DEFINING HIS DAUGHTER

As the Father and the head of the household, you define your daughter. You are her role model, her caregiver, and her teacher. Clear definitions given by a Father to his daughter give her the foundation for confidence and success in adulthood. This is the beginning of her finding her own voice.

When you esteem her, affirm her, and praise her, you create a daughter who is responsive, bright, confident, and unafraid of the challenges that will surely come her way for the rest of her life.

Claudette Wassil-Grimm, a writer and media commentator on family psychology, has pointed out five specific areas in which Fathers influence a child's personality and character development:

1) *Fathers encourage independence*; they are generally less protective [than Mothers], promoting exploration and risk-taking while modeling aggressive or assertive behaviors.
2) *Fathers expand the child's horizon*; they are the link to the "outside world" through their jobs.
3) *Fathers serve as the "alternative parent"* and they can improve the quality of the Mother's parenting by reducing her stress and stepping in to give the Mother a break during a crisis.
4) *Fathers are strict disciplinarians*; they accept fewer excuses from their children and demand more of them at each stage of development.
5) *Fathers are men*; by treating their children respectfully, they can put each child at ease with other men for the rest of the child's life.[68]

Let's talk about these five points in depth, because they describe the acts of a phenomenal Dad.

As a father, when you think of your daughter's flight plans and how you will one day launch her into her purpose and destiny, you become aware that you must deliberately shift gears to take her from altitude to altitude, higher and higher; and each of these points will assist you in doing so.

As a stable force in the home, you contribute to your daughter's stability and dependability. You establish her bedtime, curfews, the clothes she is allowed to wear, and her degree of access to entertainment. You also specify the stages of her development at which she can be exposed to various outside influences. All of these things, and more, are part of your responsibility. Your stability in decision-making will go a long way toward making her feel safe and secure. You are her first model of chivalry.

Also, the way you treat her Mom is *so* important. You daughter will be tremendously impacted by the ways you show her Mother affection and by how you treat her when she is ill, brings a new baby home, or just gets overtired doing housework. Do you help in the home and help with schoolwork? Do you prepare meals and help with the laundry? It is vital to your daughter to see a balance in gender roles and to see you involved in every aspect of home life.

You, Dad, are her first link to outside influences, careers and worldviews. Her preferences for work, sports, cars, and social skills will come predominantly from you if you are the parent most engaged in outside employment.

Now, the fun part is being her first date. Learning charm from Mom is the norm, but you will teach her first course in dating. How to order from a menu, how to look at the wine list, how to make dining reservations and discuss the cuisine options—all of these come from your modeling. But the most important thing your daughter will learn from you at this time is how to be treated on a date.

My life has always been filled with high expectations, given to me by my Dad and my precious Mother. They gave me opportunities to think outside the box and see options for myself that were not then considered appropriate for women. But such aspirations were always expected in our household.

My Dad was a high achiever, and so am I.

My Dad was involved in many social and spiritual environments, and so am I.

My Mother was very active in community events, fund-raising, and missions, and so am I.

During my childhood, my family embraced civil rights activism as a way of life. We were involved in politics, voters' rights, and women's rights, all of which were topics of conversation at dinner. My parents were concerned with their children's well-being in social, political, and civic relations, and they sought to teach us every aspect they could to make us well-rounded citizens. We marched for the poor, collected funds for foundations, and protested the racial discrimination of that era, living through the social changes that abounded in the 1950s and 1960s.

In *Fathers and Families: Paternal Factors in Child Development,* Henry Biller writes that the Father's role is crucial for a daughter to become competent. He is key to his daughter's development of assertiveness and independence. Fathers foster daughters who are achievement-oriented.

Biller is among the scholars who agree that: "positive Father-daughter relationships forge women who successfully venture into careers not typically dominated by women."[69]

I certainly agree with the research, which is now conclusive in my own life. Phenomenal Dads give their daughters wings that will take them to unparalleled achievements. I am a living testimony to this reality.

PRESENT IN HER LIFE

In large part, the Father defines his daughter by being present and attentive.

I can't remember *not* knowing my Dad, but I can remember always sitting on his lap. I have a picture of Daddy holding me in my Mom's beauty shop, and I have a photo of my Dad and Mom sitting on the couch with me when I was a baby. Those pictures say a lot. They tell me that my Daddy held me a lot and that he changed my diaper. He *did* those things.

My Daddy, he was *the guy*. He would take me to get ice cream and take me to play baseball. I always had a ball in my hand. He let me drive; in fact, he started my driving lessons when I was about five, letting me stand up in his lap to work the steering wheel. Although I didn't know it, he was building trust just by spending time with me: talking with me, investing time with me, being there. (I'll explain the importance of trust to discipline shortly.)

My Dad took me to Tiger Stadium down on Michigan Avenue. I learned all the Detroit Tigers' names, such as Rickey, Rocky Cala, Dennis Brown, Willie Horton, Bill Freehan, and the pitchers. I knew about Gates Brown because I knew his stats. He would come up to bat and we'd say, "Look, there he is." I was up there eating hot dogs; I was just hanging out with my Daddy.

I remember going to the fair with him and eating hamburgers and cotton candy. I got so sick that day. Mama asked him, "What did you feed my baby?" All the time Daddy spent with me, he was developing his touch, defining me, and nurturing me through togetherness.

ESTABLISHING ORDER AND BOUNDARIES

My Father was not a loud man. Dad didn't say a lot. But he wasn't shy or quiet; he just wasn't a big talker. But when he said something, he was very clear with just a few words.

He was so different from my Mother. Mama would be up on top of the table, the refrigerator, and everything else, and she would give you nine examples of what could happen. She'd break words down and give you the definitions. If I was doing something stupid and crazy, my Mother could "go off" if I pushed her. She wasn't a squirrely kind of a woman if she got going. When she was hot with me, she'd say, "You get your tail in here," and I would get a speech.

My Daddy would say just one sentence. He would walk by me and say, "Now get still." He'd never stop walking. But it was very clear that he meant, "Settle down!" He would never yell it. "Get still," he'd say, quietly and deliberately. I don't even know if Mama heard him. But his statements were so very clear. The moment he spoke, I felt the boundaries surround me. I knew I had pushed the envelope far enough.

Mama would negotiate; Daddy wouldn't. He would say thus, and thus, and thus, and I'd say, "But Daddy, so and so," and he'd say, "This is not a discussion."

This is a form of setting boundaries. "This is not a discussion." The words a Father uses, his tone, and his follow-through with enforcing the boundaries he sets are the foundation for a woman's ability to know and respond to a man's voice. This is one of the most astonishing aspects of a daughter's development, and it is a crucial component to her success in the marketplace.

When a girl learns the sound of her Father's voice and the authority behind it, it instills in her courage and balance; she knows when to walk with authority and when to release it; when to be emotional and when to be logical; when to be optimistic and when to be pragmatic. She can transfer this awareness to the boardroom, classroom, or any other venue. She knows the sound of a man's voice and is not afraid of it or intimidated by it. She knows the voice of authority, the tone of finality. A woman who knows her Father's voice of authority will be able to have a productive career because she can walk into the middle of any situation, and know when to discuss, when to listen and when to implement.

Dad's discipline instills trust. Remember, women were made to be responders. By nature, when a woman is guided by an authority who has her best interest in mind, she responds to him as a team member, appropriately, because she recognizes and trusts leadership.

I trusted my Father because he provided security, he taught and nurtured me, and he invested his time in me. My

Father meant good for me, not evil. My Daddy would never put me in a compromising position. I trusted him. I was grounded and stable, and that didn't come from fear of punishment. It came from trust. I was a responder to his leadership.

If a woman hasn't been violated, her response is always going to be godly: "To the pure, all things are pure. But to the one whose conscience has been defiled, nothing is pure."

As the Father, you are the first line of defense for your daughter's purity.

A good Father defines his role by loving his daughter and keeping her pure. He is to help keep her conscience pure so that she is not defiled in any way, and to allow her natural "responder" to work. When you keep your daughter pure, she doesn't have to operate out of fear of punishment. The boundaries my Father set were for my own good. They caused me to be safe and they caused me to retain my purity, so I trusted him. "Do your homework. This is not a discussion." I trusted him; I did my homework. "Go in and help your Mother." I trusted and obeyed.

Girls who do not come under a Father's discipline turn into women who do a lot of spinning. They have to do a lot of contemplation before they can make a move. The Father who sets absolutes takes away a lot of the confusion. He takes the hard part into his hands. The Father is giving her skills to implement. Without boundaries set by a Father, a daughter, since she is a child, will think she has options. But she either doesn't have real options, or she has so many that it will take the rest of her life to decide among all of them. Such a daughter can end up with nothing. She needs absolutes, rules, and authority during her childhood, adolescence, and pre-adulthood.

"This is not a discussion."

This statement is a mandate. This statement is a boundary. It says, "I'm setting a boundary for you that I'm not going to move."

A Dad who loves his daughter frequently declares rather than discusses. My Daddy once told me, "By the time I get set to talk to you, my mind's already made up."

He was doing what phenomenal Fathers are supposed to do: setting boundaries and standing by them while also loving and affirming tenderly, yet with strength.

DISCIPLINES AND CORRECTS

I kept pushing the limits. That's what daughters do. I kept fooling around with rules and modifying them when I felt I could, and after a while I crossed boundaries that were already in place. I learned the hard way that a Father can't parent without setting some consequences for breaking his rules.

You can't parent without using discipline, and you can't parent without administering consequences. You need to do a little bit of both. Discipline is redemptive: I'm redeeming you by instructing you and giving you time to turn this around. Consequences are punitive: You have broken the law and will now be punished. Discipline is the setting and teaching of standards. Consequences occur when those standards are crossed.

"This is going to hurt me more than it hurts you," is a cliché that comes alive when you have to correct your child. But you have a responsibility to discipline, which includes teaching, equipping, and training. And, yes, discipline means you also have a responsibility to administer consequences when your child breaks your rules. Your heart will sometimes hurt when you have to do this, both for what is about to happen and for what would happen if you didn't follow through.

So get over the heaviness of heart and discipline your daughter. Lovingly correct her and then affirm her, so she will know both before and afterward that she is loved, adored, and esteemed. Never let a disciplinary moment come from anger, frustration or wrath; let it always be driven by love and affection. Your daughter will come to know the difference between discipline, punishment, and abuse, if your handling of these difficult moments always begins and ends with love.

It's important that the Father not be alone in disciplining and punishing the child. The parents need to be in agreement, even though the Father may take the lead in communicating the boundaries to the child. Parents should be in agreement as they both make the rules, even though they may alternate for times of discipline. Your daughter needs to know that each parent supports the other.

My Mother was a godly woman, and she devoted herself to being a great responder to my Dad. She worked in agreement with my Father. They made the guidelines together and we *all* abided by them. But she didn't tolerate any foolishness from her children or her husband. I remember so well how she could bring order out of chaos:

In the early days, my Dad was a smoker, and she lit into him once when she caught me lighting a cigarette after he had taught me how. He quit smoking that same day.

Mama let Daddy be the leader-servant-provider, at least in my sight. She let him mete out the consequences and she definitely advocated for him. There was always mutual support between them. When your wife is advocating for you with your children, being a phenomenal Dad gets easier. You are not alone.

Did your Mother ever tell you or your siblings, "I'm going to tell your Father," or "Wait till your Father gets home."? Did that put fear in you? It did in me. When Mama said, "I'm going to tell your Father," I knew it could go one of two ways for me. Either I was in trouble, and things would go very badly for me; or someone had messed with me, and things would go well for me, but not so well for whomever my Mother had identified as a detriment.

When I was little, we had neighbors Dad didn't want me to associate with. He told me never to go into their yard. He knew so much more than I did about people and dangers and whom to associate with and whom not to, that he said, "Don't you *ever* go over there."

We were a kind of bourgeois, middle-class working family in Detroit. We would come home from school and put our school clothes away and then put our play clothes on. Not everybody had two sets of clothes. We were lucky. Like I said, I thought we were rich. We had play clothes and a garage and grass in the yard. The neighbors didn't. They had no grass, just a dirt yard separated from ours by a fence.

The neighbor girl was playing with a ball and asked if I wanted to play. Just home from school, I was wearing a pretty little pink dress, and I knew I shouldn't go. But I went anyway, though my Daddy had told me not to. The little girl immediately threw the ball on me and got my dress dirty. I started crying, but she threw the ball at me again and again. By now I was bawling.

Mama was in the basement of our house, working in her beauty shop. When she heard me, she came running out in an instant, gathered me up, and took me home. She then made me take a bath and lie down until my Dad came home.

Once he got home, my Mama told him that I had been over in the neighbor's yard, where I had had an upsetting experience and gotten my nice dress dirty.

I was naturally wondering what my Dad would do when he realized that I had disobeyed him by going next door when he had told me not to, even though I had already paid for that disobedience in several ways. He had established a clear boundary—literally the fence at the property line between our yard and the neighbors'—and I had crossed it. He was a godly man, a man who loved me, and he fulfilled his duty as a phenomenal Father by correcting me through a simple conversation the next morning at the breakfast table.

I never went next door again.

One night after church when I was fifteen, I found myself in the throes of a real confrontation with my Dad. He wasn't perfect, but I wasn't either. So we had already had some confrontations. Yet this time, my Dad and I got into a terrible standoff. It seems that as a teenager, you have to have that one last stand, that one last confrontation with your Dad. This was mine.

But before I begin telling you about it, I must tell you that there are some things about it that I don't want to share, because sometimes Fathers do lose it. Even a phenomenal Father can lose it.

Again, it was over a boy (the story of my life). This boy, somebody's nephew, had come to town and I had fallen in love with him and was planning to run away with him. I don't know where we would have gone; he was from Buffalo, New York, so maybe I thought I was going to run away to Buffalo. My seven-year-old sister and I shared a room with twin beds, and under mine was a little suitcase I had already started to pack for my getaway.

I was a real agitation to my Father at this time. He had done such a good job of protecting me, and now I was doing everything I could to mess things up. I was so full of myself as a teenager, very much pushing all the limits I could. I was sneaking around, lying, telling stories, and breaking rules, like getting on the telephone with boys when I wasn't supposed to be on the phone. All of this was very hard for my Dad, and my Mother was upset as well. I was just getting crazy.

On the night of the big confrontation, our family had just come home from church. My sister and I were in our room and we started bickering. When my sister said something I didn't like, I said, "You're lying."

Now, we couldn't say the word "lie" in our house. "Lie" and "liar" were forbidden words for us children, and I never heard my parents use them either.

My sister ran out of our room and yelled, "Daddy, Corletta said a bad word!" My Daddy came right in, still hot from hollering at me about something else. He said, "What's wrong with you, Corletta? You have just lost your mind."

"Daddy, what you talking about?" I replied.

I was already pushing, and I wasn't taking this now. I started giving him tit for tat, letting him know I had a packed suitcase under the bed and that I was ready to go off and be an adult. I was disrespectful to my Dad in the worst way.

"So you think you're grown? OK, then, you can get out!" Daddy hollered.

I was so bold and proud and stupid. I walked over to the bed and pulled the suitcase out from under it. Then I started walking to the closet to get the rest of my clothes.

That's when my Father grabbed me and spun me around. He had had it; I had pushed him beyond *his* limits!

My sister was freaking out, screaming and calling for Mama. She had tattled on me, but she didn't expect her revelation to produce such a controversy. "Mama, Mama!" she cried. My Mama came in screaming, too. "Daddy, what are you doing?"

He just lost it. I mean, he really lost it.

Oh, I cried, I cried all night.

Daddy never violated me in any way, but I remember that this particular situation put a serious breach in my heart. I had trusted him all my life, and now, for a short time, I questioned that trust. How could he have hurt me so badly?

I wish I had asked my Dad more about that incident before he died. He apologized a million times, but it was strange in the house for a while. He didn't waver, though, even though I was mad at him for a couple of years. I had trusted him from my Mother's womb. But boys had gotten into the picture, and I had constantly overstepped the boundaries Daddy had set.

I also suffered the consequences. Correction had already taken place and now discipline had taken place, too, but it wasn't working. As a result of this big confrontation, I ran smack dab into punishment.

Dad meted out the punishment for my crimes, and I thought it was too much. I thought it was more than it should have been. But I believe it worked out for my own good in spite of what I thought at the time. I came around, and I got through junior high school and into high school without any additional incidents. That confrontation had changed me. I was quieter. I stopped pushing those buttons.

Although I didn't see it then, my Mother was pivotal in defining what had happened, and without making me bitter toward my Father. She talked to me and explained what I had done and why Dad had been so upset.

And the beautiful thing was that my Father never stopped loving me. He never stopped providing for me. He never stopped taking me to school. When I turned 16, I had a car to drive to school. His love for me never changed.

You know, when you're not ready to fly solo but start telling yourself you are and think you're so smart, all that adolescent energy can become deviant. It's funny to me now when I think of myself at that age. But it wasn't funny then.

As a Father, you have to be very careful as your daughter grows into adolescence because her sexuality needs protection. And you have to know when your daughter's sexuality is sprouting. Some girls sprout early; some sprout late. A Father has to be very careful. You have to pay close attention so you will notice when that sexuality starts to blossom.

You will also have to be strong enough to walk through a season of silence if necessary. Your daughter will probably go through times when she doesn't like you. How will you deal with that when you're still teaching her how to fly?

I believe there are lots of times when Fathers hold back because they would rather get applause from a daughter than deal with her anger over a punishment, or even over basic discipline.

In *Fly Away Home*, whenever Amy got mad at her Dad, she'd go out and be alone with her geese. As a phenomenal Father, you have to be prepared for the seasons of silence when your daughter thinks you're the meanest man in the world. I thought my Dad was the meanest man in the world the day of that big confrontation. And I grew silent for a while.

So you have to be OK with a season or two of silence. You still have to be a Father: loving, providing, and protecting. When your daughter goes silent on you because she thinks you're too severe, don't react. Don't get angry or punitive, and don't withdraw or isolate yourself, either. Just keep loving her. Keep talking to her. Keep reaching out to her. You still have to love her!

Keep talking. That's what my Father did when I shut down. Keep providing, keep talking, and keep sitting at the table with her. Don't let her stay in her room or get an attitude and start stomping off. Keep the lines open. Keep your eyes on your daughter.

My Father continued to communicate with me. He never withdrew; he never treated me funny. After our biggest confrontation, he came and apologized the next day. That incident hurt me for years, but he said it hurt him more than it hurt me, and it probably did.

As a child, you think you know what's best, but you don't. I can even laugh now at the episode my sisters call my "big beat-down." Daddy never changed after the encounter. After I got over my initial mortification and self-pity, my trust was higher than before. I continued to honor my Father.

When you are a phenomenal Dad, you will have an awareness of your daughter's timetables. When she isn't ready to fly, you will need to stiffen up, but you will be ensuring that your little girl is fully prepared for life's flight as she grows. If she's getting real love from her Dad, she gets to continue being Daddy's girl, not some boyfriend's sexual playmate. She learns what healthy, respectful love is from her Dad, and she also learns how to conduct herself among men.

The first time I went to a movie, my Father took me. The first time I went to a fancy restaurant, my Father took me. The first time I got dressed up to go out, it was with my Father. My Father opened doors for me. He gave me a model of how a gentleman behaves in the presence of a lady.

In the 1960s, I reached the age that he would let a boy come to see me. The boys would pull up and blow their car horns. My Daddy would go out to meet them and say, "You don't pull up at this house and blow your horn to pick up my girl. Get out of the car." They had to come inside. "Sit down; let's talk," my Daddy would say then. If a boy came to visit, he had to sit in the living room with me while my Daddy sat at the dining room table reading the paper.

That's the sort of thing you do for your daughter. You show her that you are her leader, provider, and protector.

Most Dads are embarrassed about doing that. In many cases, they hand over the oversight of dating to their wives. They let the Mother do it.

Other Dads try to be buddies with the boyfriends, instead of teaching them how to treat their daughter. My Father was more concerned with determining where the boys' heads were at. My Mother told me one day, "When a man comes into a room, another man knows it." My Father was a man, and he wanted to know what kind of man had come to date his daughter—a gentleman or a boy.

RESPECTING HER MOTHER

Your wife, your daughter's Mother, is someone's daughter. She's a daughter who is now flying with you, Dad. Your own daughter needs to see, hear and experience you respecting this other daughter, who is now her Mother.

As a male, you'll always be encountering someone's daughter. She could be your own Mother; she could be your daughter; she could be your wife. But she is always somebody's daughter. That means you will always have the care of someone's daughter, even if she's not yours. Your sweetheart is somebody's daughter.

My Daddy would come home and have a nice, quiet dinner with us; we always ate dinner and breakfast together as family. My Mother always cooked breakfast and she always cooked dinner. So my Daddy never ate out, and that's something he was proud of. When I was a teenager, he told me, "Baby, when you get married, feed your husband at home. Feed him good and he won't have room for Jello."

Jello commercials were always on TV at that time, but I had to grow up a little to know what he actually meant. (You might have to think about it, as well, to get his real meaning.)

Consistently preparing home-cooked meals for him was one of the ways my Mom responded to my Dad, because he was such a good role model. He wasn't just a good Dad; he was a good husband. He treated my Mother as well as he treated me. She responded by saying such things as, "Hey, he's home!" She had dinner ready every night and breakfast ready every morning. She worked every day, too; she had her own beauty shop. She was an entrepreneur, and as more

153

children came along, she also took a night job. But she never stopped responding to my Dad. As he grew older, she took care of him at home until he died.

My Father modeled loving leader and provider behavior and my Mother modeled loving response.

Men, your daughter is—or will be—a Mother; your Mother is a daughter; your wife is a Mother *and* a daughter. Respect your Father-in-law's daughter—your wife. You are tasked by God to nurture her. And assume a loving Father-leader-provider mentality toward *all* the women in your life. Every woman you encounter is someone's daughter. Speak kindly to all of these women. You owe each of them respect, the same respect you should be showing your own daughter.

My husband recently said something very powerful:

"Men, don't ever send your wife to the door. If it rings, go get it. If the AC is too cold in the night, don't let her get out of the bed to turn it down. You do it. Let her know that she can wake you up when she's cold, and that you'll be the one to get up and adjust the temperature. And put the groceries up when she buys them. You might make the most money, but don't put everything else off on her."

He was talking about responsibility. He was talking about the man's role as provider-leader-giver. The head-of-household mandate for men, which is from God, is not a license to boss people around, though it's been misconstrued that way throughout history.

So don't make your women work for you. Work for them. And let your children see you do it. Maybe your wife buys the groceries, but when it's time to bring them into the house, don't you let her touch a single bag. And don't be afraid to work for your children as well. Do that all the time.

My husband was right on with what he said. The man's role is to be leader, provider, giver, and servant. My husband is always on his watch for those in his care, and you should do the same.

TAKEAWAYS

- In what ways do you see yourself as a phenomenal Father?
- In what ways do you think you can improve?
- Are you treating your wife like someone's daughter? Do your children see this?

Teach Your Daughters to Fly

CHAPTER 9

Permission to Stay Behind

"You go ahead, I'm fine. You can do this."

In *Fly Away Home*, the Dad crashes his own plane and in a very emotional moment makes the decision to have his daughter finish her mission without him. He has gone with her as far as he can and now decides to stay behind.

It takes a big man to lift his daughter to the top while he remains in the shadows of her success and at his own level of achievement.

As her Father, you nurture her, deposit time and energy for her education and well-being, give her skills, and teach her to fly.

Eventually it will be time to stand back and watch others applaud her, but she'll look across the room and catch your eye, affirming you. She will know then how much you taught her. She may not get on every stage and call your name, but if you're in the audience, she'll give you that look that says she knows.

Amy becomes a celebrity *after* her Dad crashes; it only happens when he refuses to fly on with her to her final destination. When your daughter has the confidence that she can do something, she will do it; and she will do it *better and longer. She'll go farther, and she'll get the attention you never did as her Father.*

Releasing your daughter for her first solo takeoff is really about affirmation. It's about your confidence in yourself as a coach, mentor and Father. So this part is about you, Dad. When you permit yourself to release her, to let her go on without you, that permission will allow her to fly her own plane.

So, in spite of the butterflies in your stomach and the panic in your heart, when the moment comes to let go, you must release her. If you don't, you'll cripple her, possibly for the rest of her life.

When the time for letting go arrives, remember that you've given her the ability to make good decisions. You've given her boundaries, taught her how to add and subtract, taught her the ABCs of life, and taught her to respect authority. You've taught her everything you know. Now you must trust the model you've given her. It's time to step back and stop leading. It's time to let her fly.

Although she'll still hear your voice, she will hear other voices too. Some of them will be those of other men, who will influence her and the decisions she must make. You don't want to snatch her back just to make yourself comfortable; now's the time to really trust her instincts, and to trust her ability to think for herself. If you don't do that now, she may never be able to fly solo.

In *Fly Away Home*, it's very important that the script calls for the Dad's plane to crash. I think that's so vital. He doesn't land willingly. He doesn't instinctively know when to stop flying beside his daughter. It takes a mechanical failure of his own craft for him to know it's time to let go. Once he's on the ground, he realizes that even if he can get his own craft flying again, it would hinder Amy for the rest of her life. He has taken her as far as he can take her, and she now needs permission to soar on her own. But he must first give himself permission to remain on the ground while she flies away. And so he does.

You see, giving your daughter permission to go is about you, Dad.

In 1985, at the family meeting in which my Dad said, "I'm going to turn the family business over to you," with tears running down his face, he was releasing his legacy into my hands. I know he had looked over all of his children to see which one could best lead and command the respect of the others so that they would follow. He was just that logical. He didn't just make a random call; he considered that important moment again and again before he ever summoned me.

I remember looking into his eyes after he announced his decision. Although I saw the greatest look of confidence in them, I ignored the tears because I didn't understand then why he was crying. It must have been excruciatingly hard for him, considering all he had put into this business that he and my Mother had built. For him to suddenly be only a silent partner in something he had founded was going to take a lot of patience from all of us, but he and I both knew his plane had run out of fuel.

I was sharper and faster than he was, and my vision was bigger. I could do the job, and he knew it.

He also knew that we couldn't fly on together in two separate aircraft, side-by-side. So he decided to join the ground team. He would flag my flight off, disengage the portable blocks, and make sure there would be no baggage carts, food trucks, or idle pedestrians blocking my pullback from the gate. He would take measures to ensure that I would not inadvertently injure anyone as I took off. Then he would let go. It was time for me to fly without him.

Not until writing this book did I realize how big a decision he had to make. At this crucial moment, he was setting me up for success. He trusted that everything he had taught me—and all I had seen of his leadership and emulated—would now be well executed. He would sit back and celebrate my successes, with the hope that I would give him his due honor.

Dad, letting go of your daughter is probably the hardest thing you'll ever do. It is so difficult for most men that when they hold on too long, it prevents their daughters from having healthy and wholesome relationships with other men. Knowing when to give yourself permission to stand down gives your daughter the confidence she needs to proceed— with her own life, her own career, and her own family— without having to compete with her Father.

If under your tutelage and watchful eye a bond has been established, then the bond now must be rearranged, reimagined and reconfigured. Under ideal conditions, this bonding between Father and daughter will last a lifetime. But it will now go from one way of expression to something totally different. In her early years you were always there. Now that she is older, the bond remains, but your positioning is different. You're no longer side-by-side; now you watch from afar. You're there if she needs you, but she will be the one to discover that need and reach out to you.

The permission I refer to in this chapter is not about the permission you give to her. Dad, the permission you need to give now is to yourself. Give yourself permission to remain behind and watch your little girl become vested in the authority and wisdom you have entrusted to her. Permit yourself to believe that everything you've taught her is going to work, and work well.

The Father in *Fly Away Home* gives himself that permission. It will compromise the mission if he tries to get his plane fixed to resume flying with his daughter. To meet the deadline he has to let her go on by herself. He needed to stay back, stay on the ground, and meet her at her destination.

It's going to be tough to let your daughter go, to relinquish your leadership. But it's the next step on her flight plan, flying solo and going the distance without you.

In a traditional wedding ceremony, the Father walks his daughter down the aisle, and at the beginning of the vows, there's a point that requires the Father to release his daughter to another man. At that moment, the Dad is saying, "I give her to you, to be your wife."

That's the most obvious interpretation. But what I'm saying to you, Dad, is that you should be saying, "I give myself permission not to be to her what I've been all of my life."

So when the Father says, "I give her away," he is actually saying, "My tenure of being the leading man in my daughter's life is completed."

This is hard.

You have to give yourself permission not to rescue your daughter from this point forward. Don't fix their plumbing, mow their yard, or step in as superhero once she is married, since such things often cause conflict between Dad and husband.

In *Fly Away Home*, Thomas Alden knows that if he goes back up in his plane, his daughter won't fly by herself. She'll never know what she can do on her own if he doesn't stay on the ground.

Dad, once you refuse to go any further, your daughter can fly, soar, and be a celebrity; now she can get the attention. She can now get everything you taught her to get, but she'll never get those things until you "crash" and refuse to get up.

In the movie, Thomas gives Amy the ultimate permission: to fly on her own, un-chaperoned, as leader of the pack. Thomas has crashed his little plane. He is OK; he isn't hurt or unable to carry on, but he cannot continue this flight. This is Amy's chance to discover her own strength, and her Dad wants her to do it.

When he tells her to fly on without him, she panics. "I can't find my way without you," she says.

"Yes, you can," Thomas answers, exhorting her to use the strength within her.

"I can't leave you here," Amy pleads.

"Yes, you can. You take that plane, those geese, and you fly away."

"Bye, Dad," she says.

He has only one more word to say, and he says it now: "Go!" Knowing he has given his daughter the skills she needs, he releases himself from the obligation of flying with her the rest of the way to fulfill her mission.

Unfortunately, fear prevents many Dads from releasing their daughters; it stops them from stepping back. So many women have never been released to be the best they can be. Their Fathers died, or their Fathers abandoned their Mothers, or their Fathers didn't do what they were supposed to do, or they didn't say what they were supposed to say. So many Dads have missed that critical moment in time when their aircraft needed to be grounded.

Timing is critical here. This moment will come only once, and to know it, feel it and execute it takes *real* courage. It comes at no particular age for either the Dad or the daughter. Mission and purpose trump in priority over age. The moment will come when your daughter's mission is apparent and staring at you. She's groomed and prepared, maybe a little scared, but within her she already has what it takes for a safe takeoff. She's ready, but are you?

Why is this moment so very important in your life as a Dad?

It's important because you never want to be known as a controller who makes all the decisions for her. You don't want to make your daughter a codependent woman, and you don't want to make your daughter your wife.

Most codependent parents expect a level of devotion and love from their child that is unhealthy and unnatural. It's expected to make up for that which they lack in other relationships. This is how a relationship between Dad and his daughter can become toxic and lead to unhealthy expectations and benchmarks that last a lifetime. The worst thing you can do is to *not* give yourself permission to release her—to make her dependent on you by clipping her wings.

Dad, when you give yourself permission to release your daughter, just lay back and let her go; you are posturing her for the best life she can live. You are saying to her, "You can do this without me now!"

Long after you're gone, she might write a book like this, one that will give you, her Dad all the credit, and people will wish they had had the opportunity to meet you. Don't cripple your daughter by flying too long beside her.

Don't make her weak.

Don't limit her to your altitude. Her plane is bigger, her wings are wider, and her vision is broader.

Finally, know when to stop. Know when to land, and know when to tell her to go.

TAKEAWAYS

- In your relationship with your daughter, was there a time when you should have stepped back and didn't? What did you do?
- Are you comfortable when you are not in the limelight of your daughter's success?
- What do you need to do to prepare for your own success after you release your daughter?

CHAPTER 10

●●●

You're a Natural!

"I've been around a lot of flyers in my time," Thomas Alden calls to his daughter, Amy, who is about to take off. "I think you're a natural."
"Do you really think so?" Amy yells back, beaming.

Dad, when you look at your daughter, remember that you are looking at a potential world leader, not just your little girl that you love and adore. And as you look at your wife, your sister, or your Mother, remember that you are looking at leadership in a skirt.

According to the author of a Forbes.com article, women held more than 51 percent of managerial and professional positions in 2011.[70] The same author states that women excel at discovering opportunities, networking, developing relationships, and giving.[71]

"Women may be more productive and more profitable in business. *Women are naturally wired to think, act, and innovate…. Women, more than men, have the ability to see what others don't, to do what others won't, and to keep pushing their ideas and ideals when prudence says to quit."*

Women are natural leaders.

"You're a natural," Thomas Alden says to his daughter in *Fly Away Home* as he puts her in her aircraft and sends her on her way.

Women are leaders and multi-taskers; they are highly collaborative in the home and marketplace. I know many women who are knowledge-seekers, positioning themselves for the landscape of decision-makers while living balanced lives.

So, Dad, you have been given a daughter to raise, and you must prepare her for the world that awaits her. Your daughter is a diamond; don't undervalue her or penalize her because she's a female. Dad, you have access to the next world leader, scientist, CEO, president, political mover and shaker, radio announcer, TV host, religious leader, or head of state. Her options are endless. The mission your daughter is a natural for may surprise you, but once you identify what it is, it becomes your job to develop her for success in that area.

A leadership study conducted to examine women's corporate leadership effectiveness found that for the sixteen competency areas covered, *female leaders scored significantly higher than men in ten of those areas.* The survey sought feedback from the business associates, employees and supervisors of 16,000 business leaders. On average, thirteen people responded for each leader surveyed.

Women scored highest in: taking initiative, displaying high integrity and honesty, driving for results, practicing self-development, and developing others. They scored higher in: inspiring and motivating, building relationships, collaboration and teamwork, championing change and establishing goals. Women also scored higher in solving problems and analyzing issues, and even in communicating powerfully and prolifically.[72]

The woman was created as a leader, given dominion *along* with man by God in the beginning to subdue, dominate and multiply. She gives birth. Not only can she conceive a baby; she can carry it, protect it, and birth it. And without any additional support, she can also nourish it. That's leadership.

As a Father, you play a vital role in recognizing your daughter's natural proclivities. Once you identify how she is wired, you must then connect the wires and the proper sockets so that her purpose will shine forth. Your daughter was created to do almost everything that you can do, and most times better than you, Dad. A woman withstands more, goes through more, endures more, and expects less. Can you imagine, Dad, going through forty-one hours of labor to birth a child?

So your daughter is a natural leader. But what happens when there are children of both genders in the home? In many cases, Fathers have built-in prejudice and show preference for male children. They think, "My son is going to be greater than my daughter." Even today, in some countries, a daughter may be killed if she is the firstborn. The son is "auto-leader" based solely on his genitali–not on his brain, his skill or his strategic thinking ability, but on his sex. The girl is discounted and in some cases punished solely because she's a girl.

Dad, in your daughter's heart, there is a silent cry for you to see her natural abilities and celebrate her for having them.

When Thomas Alden tells his daughter to lean over in her plane during her training-to-fly stage, she just leans; it's easy for her. She's a natural, and he tells her so.

Women are naturals; they're not *trying* to be stronger. In a conflict, they can jump right in as mediators. A Mother who has never studied medicine can heal her child. She will know what to pick up, whether it's aspirin or mustard or a foul-smelling poultice. She knows how to bring a child's health back. She asks the right questions. She has the right remedies. And when she steps into leadership, her role is more discerned than learned.

So don't despise your daughter's natural instincts. Your son might not be your best successor. He may not be the "junior" you're looking for. There's an idea that if your son carries your name, he also carries your strengths. That's not necessarily so. Your daughter may carry your strengths while your son carries your name! *If you have a son, there's no guarantee that he will do well as your successor. Your daughter might just be a better natural leader than your son.*

After all, women have been running households for all of human history. What is more corporate than a household? And who runs it?

Everything that goes into the infrastructure of a corporation is in the home: management, underlings, fiscal affairs, human resources, health care, nutrition, education, and housekeeping. Who runs all of that? If you are married, your wife does, and she will show your daughter the imagery of marriage and the posture of a leader.

Women are more perceptive and able to anticipate, while men have to be told detail after detail. Women think on their feet, without pre-knowledge of details. They're more spiritual and have good antennae for faith and prayer; and they're more open to dialogue that doesn't come from facts, statistics, logic, or data.

So, Dad, stop overlooking your daughter's natural instincts, perceptions and ability to lead.

How many homes are led by women? Remember, the home is the very first and most major corporation on the earth.

According to the 2012 U.S. Census Report, 25.8 percent of all children in the United States are being raised by a single parent, compared with an average of 14.9 percent in other countries.[73] But in the African American community, 72 percent of the children are being raised in a single-parent household, with the overwhelming majority of them led by women.[74]

The trend toward single-parent households is due to the prevalence of children born outside marriage. It has been increasing since record keeping began. It spiked up in the 1970s and 1980s and has never gone down.

About 40 percent of U.S. children today—about four out of every ten—are born to unwed Mothers, with 80 percent of these children being raised by the Mother alone, according to the U.S. Census Bureau. The overwhelming majority—about two-thirds—of these unwed Moms are under thirty-years-old. And sadly, about half of their children live in poverty.[75]

Many women raising children alone are doing so with limited resources, which is a major undertaking all by itself. Given the lack of "bells and whistles" commonly found in traditional, two-parent families, this accomplishment bespeaks the natural instinct of women to lead, provide, and protect.

Women have earned close to ten million more college degrees than men since 1982. What's more, many women earned those degrees while working, keeping up a home, caring for children and transporting them to and from school, and, from time-to-time, going out on a date.[76] It's not hard for a woman to juggle many assignments at one time and do them all fairly well.

A female leader is more likely to be authentic as a person and less competitive in the marketplace than a man. Although her primary affirmation isn't primarily based on competition or challenge, her expertise often expands out of gratitude for the opportunity. This is her best motive and the drive behind her successes.

A woman has natural perception and instinct, often seeing a problem before any of her male counterparts do. And when she sees the conflict, she also tends to know just what's needed before the due diligence data hits her desk.

She sees, hears, and knows without any shadows or contradictions in perception. Once she determines the legitimacy behind the opportunity, she is postured to perform.

Many men feel that they are in competition with their wives and resent their skills and successes. Such men will also despise leadership instincts in their daughters. The way a man's Mother appeared to him when he was a child may also distort the way he cares for his wife and daughters.

Marital tension can create a culture of fear, not respect, in the hearts of the children. A competition may ensue, and the mindset that some men reach is, "I'm going to prove you're wrong."

A daughter sees this and may take up the challenge to be strong no matter how her Mother is being treated. But she might also become silent and lose her voice, fearing that your criticism of her Mother will become her experience as well. She could then go the rest of her life without expressing an opinion. Too many daughters see that they are not rewarded for expressing their views and that their Mothers are mistreated when they speak their mind.

Such a daughter learns to be quiet, muzzled, and miserable. Don't let this happen to your daughter, Dad!

My Dad was a special man, and daughters are dear to their Dads. At the time he was getting ready to arrange the succession of the family business, none of my brothers were prepared, positioned, or perceptive enough to see the value of what Daddy was going to leave. As the firstborn, I was the immediate candidate, and, thank God, my Father did not overlook my natural instincts and abilities to carry the legacy forward. None of my brothers wanted the leadership spot, nor did they want to be involved with the business after I was named CEO.

My sisters and I have since labored to build what is now a global non-profit from the seedling of our parents' loving labor. My sisters didn't try to force my brothers to "take over or else." They saw that I was prepared and ready. With my natural perception, eagerness to serve diligently and learn the business, I was able to fill a spot in our industry not commonly filled by a woman.

Even now, people sometimes ask me, "Why did your Father give his business to you? What made him choose you?"

The answer is that he chose me because he knew I'm a natural. I was ready to jump in and be grateful for the opportunity, and he wanted me to have that opportunity, no matter what anyone else said.

Fathers should not choose their sons over their daughters just because of gender. Your daughter has natural leadership abilities. Your wife has natural leadership abilities. If your son is gifted, use him, but never deny your daughter a chance simply because she is female. What matters is the ability to discern who is best for an assignment. Who's best at leading? Who's a natural for it?

What are your daughter's natural gifts and talents? Is she good at something specific? Does she have a good eye? Is she a good decorator or dresser? Is she good at arrangements? Does she have an engineering mind? Is she

174

good at perception and anticipation? Can she find resolutions or solutions for hard issues and questions? Can she make things simple? Is she good at resolving conflict? Is she patient? Can she go the distance? Does she have endurance?

Usually she has 100 times more of some of these qualities than a man does. If she's sick, she still has to cook with a baby on her hip. She's still going to do it. Multitasking probably comes easily to her; in fact, she probably doesn't have to think about it twice.

Encourage your daughter to lead.

That's what I saw Amy Alden's Father do in *Fly Away Home*. He encouraged her. He didn't have to give her certain skills and attitudes; they were already in her naturally. Giving encouragement is what Dads are doing around the world, and that's what my precious Father did.

Look how many women head corporations now. In mid-2014, there were twenty-four female CEOS in the Fortune 500:[77]

CEO	Company	2014 Fortune500 Rank
Mary Barra	General Motors	7
Meg Whitman	Hewlett-Packard	17
Virginia Rometty	IBM	23
Patricia A. Woertz	Archer Daniels Midland	27
Indra K. Noovi	PepsiCo	43
Marillyn Hewson	Lockheed Martin	59
Ellen J. Kullman	DuPont	86
Irene B. Rosenfeld	Mondelez International	89

Phebe Novakovic	General Dynamics	99
Carol Meyrowitz	The TJX Companies	108
Lynn Good	Duke Energy	123
Ursula M. Burns	Xerox	137
Sheri S. McCoy	Avon	234
Deanna M. Mulligan	Guardian Life Insurance	245
Kimberly S. Bowers	CST Brands	266
Debra L. Reed	Sempra Energy	267
Barbara Rentler	Ross Stores	277
Denise M. Morrison	Campbell Soup	315
Susan M. Cameron	Reynolds American	329
Heather Bresch	Mylan	377
Ilene S. Gordon	Ingredion	412
Jacqueline C. Hinman	CH2M Hill	437
Kathleen M. Mazzarella	Graybar Electric	449
Gracia C. Martore	Gannett	481

Look at the corporations at the top of the preceding list: IBM, Xerox, Hewlett-Packard, General Motors, PepsiCo, Archer Midland Daniels, DuPont, Lockheed Martin. These are the firms that turn the wheels of the American economy. Some major companies were built by, founded by, and sustained by women. Women lead many of the largest companies in the world. And they've been far more successful than men in these jobs, in many cases.

Let's consider a few:

MEG WHITMAN

Meg Whitman worked as an executive for the Walt Disney Company, for Hasbro and for other corporations before she signed on as the CEO of the eBay Internet auction website in 1998, when she was forty. The company had thirty employees and revenues of about $4 million. Immediately, she made changes to the website and built an executive team. During her tenure as CEO, the company grew to 15,000 employees and $8 billion in annual revenue. The New York Times ran an article that included her as one person with the credentials to become president.[78] She ran for governor of California, winning her primary but losing to serial governor Jerry Brown in 2009. In 2011, she became CEO of Hewlett-Packard. Her net worth in 2013 was believed to be $1.3 billion.[79]

MARY KAY ASH

Mary Kay Ash, who passed away in 2001, epitomized pioneering spirit and leadership in spite of difficult life challenges. She married at age seventeen, had three children, and sold books door-to-door while her husband served in World War II. Divorced in 1945, Ash worked for Stanley Home Products, where she trained a man only to have him promoted over her. She began working on a business plan for her own business, and in 1963, after her second husband's death, she launched Mary Kay Cosmetics with $5,000; by 1969, she was a millionaire.

Mary Kay Cosmetics went public in 1976, but afterward, getting guff from stockholders, Ash bought back all the shares in a leveraged buyout. She founded the company, grew it, sold it, and bought it back to sustain it. Not only is Mary Kay a business founded by a woman; it's for women, to women. In 1999, one of the company's original consultants surpassed $1 million in commissions.[80] Around 100,000 consultants have won the lease of a pink Cadillac.[81] And you should see the diamonds the company is giving to its top sellers this year!

ESTEE LAUDER

Lauder was the only woman on *Time* magazine's 1998 list of the twenty most influential business geniuses of the 20th century. She was a recipient of the Presidential Medal of Freedom. As a teenager, she agreed to help her uncle, Dr. John Schotz (a chemist), with his business. His company sold beauty products, such as creams, lotions, rouge, and fragrances. She became more interested in his business than in her Father's. She was fascinated watching her uncle create his products.

After graduating from Newtown High School, she focused on her uncle's business. She named one of his blends and began selling his products to her friends. One day, as she was getting her hair done at the House of Ash Blondes, Florence Morris, the salon owner, asked Lauder about her perfect skin. Soon, she returned to the beauty parlor to hand out four of her uncle's creams and demonstrate their use. Morris was so impressed that she asked Lauder to sell her products at her new salon. In 1953, Lauder introduced her first fragrance. In its first year, it sold 50,000 bottles, and by 1984, the figure had jumped to 150 million. Explaining her success, Lauder said, "I have never worked a day in my life without selling. If I believe in something, I sell it, and I sell it hard."[82]

OPRAH WINFREY

The American Spectator says Oprah Winfrey is "arguably the most influential woman in the world."[83] *Time* magazine and CNN both call her "arguably the world's most powerful woman," and *Time* named her among "the 100 people who most influenced the 20th century" and put her on its list of the "most influential people" from 2004 to 2011. According to *Vanity Fair*, "Oprah Winfrey arguably has more influence on the culture than any university president, politician, or religious leader, except perhaps the Pope." [84]

Columnist Maureen Dowd made this assessment: "She is the top alpha female in this country. She has more credibility than the president."[85] Even pundit Bill O'Reilly said Oprah is a woman who "came from nothing to rise up to be the most powerful woman, I think, in the world … Anybody who goes on her program immediately benefits through the roof. I mean, she has a loyal following; she has credibility; she has talent; and she's done it on her own to become fabulously wealthy and fabulously powerful."[86]

Even in the business world, women are the chief influencers of how marketing and product development is done. Companies cater directly to female in their advertising, and statistics show that women directly affect up to 80 percent of all purchases.

Dad, take the *time* to discover through conversation and observation what your daughter is naturally good at in leadership. Remember that women lead very differently than their male counterparts, but they are leaders nevertheless. It can be difficult for a man to understand how women think–unless he is closely influenced by the women in his life. Women process things differently, with circular and better-rounded vision.

So when you are preparing your plan of succession, never omit your daughter as a viable candidate for leadership.

She's a natural for the job!

TAKEAWAYS

- After reading this chapter, what do you see in your daughter that you never saw or acknowledged before?

- Do you favor your son over your daughter? If so, why?

- How can you prepare your daughter for leadership?

CHAPTER 11

●●●

"Come In, Mother Goose"

"It takes a team."

As a woman, I love the movie *Fly Away Home* so much because it speaks to me, and I always learn something new every time I watch it. Who would ever have thought there could be so many lessons in a simple little Disney movie?

Dads, I'd like to talk to you about networking—about how to start your daughter on a successful flight pattern for life by involving others and allowing others to touch her dream. She first learns how to socially interact from you, her Father and patriarch. If you allow her to be a loner, a recluse, or just socially inept, you can cripple her for life.

When Thomas Alden started putting his vision into real form, a crew of people quickly assembled around him. His brother was there already, in a supporting role. Other ultralight plane enthusiasts became involved, and a young, jack-of-all-trades was loyal. Thomas's girlfriend, from whom Amy remained aloof at first, not only came on board after a brief hesitation, but also became a captain in the 1,000-mile mission. She also played a profound but subtle role as a nurturing Mother figure who ultimately helped Dad gain Amy's trust.

When a game warden appears, hurts one of Amy's geese, and then threatens to confiscate the rest of them, she concludes that her Dad must have lied to her. Then the shower malfunctions, causing Dad and a stranger to see Amy naked in the bathroom. She retreats, crying, screaming and mortified, to her crowded little room in Dad's house. This was a pretty bad day. Then Alden's girlfriend comes in to console the thirteen-year-old.

"Why did he bring a man to chop their wings off?" Amy wails.

"Your Father didn't know."

"He did, and that man is coming back!"

"No, he's not. Amy, listen to me. Listen to me! I know I can't replace your Mother. Nobody can. But if you let me, I can be your friend. The first rule of friends is: they have to trust each other. I promise you, nothing is going to happen to those geese. Nothing. I won't let it, and neither will your Dad. It's a promise."

As a team starts to assemble around her project, Amy becomes known as "Mama Goose." Her Dad, of course, is "Papa Goose," and other team members include "Ground Goose" and "Wet Goose"—the latter being the boat that tracks Amy's flight over Lake Erie.

It takes a team. "Mama Goose" needs other people to help her fly. They can monitor the weather reports for her and help her navigate from different perspectives to allow for the best decision-making along the way.

At times, her little plane has no radio reception. Nor does she have an air traffic controller. Ground Goose says, "OK, weather's heading this way," or, "Weather's heading that way." Although Amy is the one flying and soaring, and Daddy is in the air with her for part of the route, this is a team effort. When she has to fly over Lake Erie, a team member is navigating. Other team members' roles were critical before the flight began. There's Thomas's brother, who wrestles down the logistics as soon as the project seems feasible: where to fly each day; where to land each night; the duration of each layover; and pinpointing the final destination. He rustles up some maps and says, "I'll make a call, because I know this guy, a bird guy, in North Carolina. He knows, like, migratory paths ... we call him Birdbrain."

Birdbrain turns out to be the team's missing link. He finds the only 300 acres available that can sustain the birds, along a wetland corridor that's under the threat of more bulldozers.

For Amy's project to succeed, all teams player had to be in place. She knew she couldn't succeed on her own.

As I grew up, I knew there were people on my team, people who would help me get where I needed to go.

For your daughter to have her own first safe takeoffs, she will have to count on the "village" she is most familiar with: her Mom, Dad, siblings, aunts, uncles, and others.

However, as she gets older, her boundaries should expand so that others can give her the directives and support she will need for the long journey ahead.

The worse thing that can happen to a girl is to be socially challenged with outside relationships while having no mentors, teachers or support personnel to play vital roles in helping her reaching her ultimate destination. This is when Dads are so important, because they teach their daughters how to trust others. When a daughter sees her Dad trust others, when he is able to include the others in her dream and approve the way they treat her, he empowers her.

You can give your daughter a great gift: the ability to network and work with others. Having a team and knowing that you have approved it satisfies your daughter's needs for approval and companionship and gives her the long-term ability to develop lasting relationships. She will learn the value of a strong circle of support players, who can serve her well for years to come. In times of emotional weakness, physical shortages, spiritual collapse or economic uncertainty, they will help her make her flights remain successful and consistent.

Such team members are like tools in a toolbox: everyone has a specialty. Each does something extremely well; and each has things he or she doesn't do so well.

That's why networking is so important in life. The cohesion of gifts and talents makes for strong and successful outcomes for everyone involved.

Dad, as your daughter learns to listen to others and gains the courage to execute a plan that was not totally yours, her team will benefit and promote her in the marketplace in ways that formal education cannot. A woman's ability to work with others is a benchmark for leadership; and the ability to include a team is so much greater an asset when it is handed to a daughter from her Father.

A daughter's networking is a lifelong, continual process, but it begins with how you, as her Father, allow others to be included. Teach her to engage others and help her feel comfortable with having them know and share her dream. That diminishes the fear factor, and her courage will emerge when her bases are covered by faithful friends, supporters, and guides. Never be afraid to provide your daughter with good connections. That is the beginning of her lifelong networking.

Now, Dad, you must be there first!

No matter what happens between you and your wife, you are the president of your daughter's first network. You cannot be irresponsible. You cannot be absent. You must engage your daughter and not be an auxiliary parent or a hands-off Dad. You must be active in caregiving and not play a secondary role as a parent.

Even if you are divorced, or were never married to your daughter's Mother, you still cannot slack off with your presence or active parenting.

Your emotional support through involved Fatherhood is the core of your daughter's confidence, self-identity and self-reliance. Your role as a financial provider is also immensely important. *Don't be a Deadbeat Dad!*

Divorces, death and other crises are a fact of life today, but *don't disappear!* If you are absent and there is no support team, your daughter will suffer from a diminished self-concept, and her physical and emotional security will be compromised.

Children consistently report feeling abandoned when their Fathers are not involved in their lives. They struggle with their emotions and may experience episodes of self-loathing.

If your time is limited, involve other people in her life who will support her; this will always lead her to respect and love you even more. Uncles, brothers and a network of others can take the hit for your long work hours and career challenges while still providing the support she needs.

As your daughter begins to fly, as she enters the trajectory of her success, she will need her team. She will need people around her to help her to fly and arrive safely. Provide that network for her, Dad, even if some of your friends and family members reject you for doing it.

My Dad was rejected by his peers after he turned the business over to me. Many questioned his decision because he had sons. Those people thought gender alone should be the only qualifying factor for succession. But my Dad had a plan, and he knew that teaching his daughters to fly would keep the investment of his life safe, sound and secure for many years to come. When the rejection came, my Father found faithful men and women outside of my nuclear family that would support me in my flight. He introduced me to ground troops and made sure that I had some other women on board for the long-view visioning.

My Mother was also instrumental in securing the water crews and air crews. Every day brought exposure to opportunities they knew of and people who had the know-how to help me over the long-term project. My parents didn't keep my gift a secret; they told everyone they knew. They engaged family members, associates, business partners and other people who would be by my side and keep communications open for counseling direction and guidance. What a gift!

Networking has helped me until this moment, and nothing I have accomplished was achieved by being alone and flying solo. No, whatever I have achieved, it took teamwork to make it a reality. Here's what my Dad provided for me:

- Strong female role models.
- Other leaders in our specialized field.
- Family friends.
- People with substance, finances, resources, influence and relationships.
- Spiritual guides.
- Mentors and teachers.

In selecting your daughter's support team, use mixed genders, because both bring a unique energy to any team, and your daughter will learn the value of both men's and women's talents.

All of these people will make a great ground team for a daughter's journey and success. Each will bring a wealth of support, knowledge, and wisdom to her life, and inspire her to go the distance. We all need people that we can model ourselves after and journey with. For a young, impressionable girl, selecting the right team is vital, so that she will have the rght people to admire and encourage her along the way.

Her social skills will make the difference in the marketplace. As your daughter leads and others follow, she will thank you for putting her team together early and making it possible for her to have a lifetime of successes.

Papa Goose, good job!

TAKEAWAYS

- Who in your daughter's life is currently part of her ground and air crew?
- Who do you need to add in order to help her achieve her destiny?
- How will you handle the rejection that may come your way as you support your daughter?

CHAPTER 12

●●●

Against All Odds

"What are the odds that geese will migrate south following a young girl in a large aircraft painted to look like them?"

"4 days beyond our schedule, no permits, no flight plans; we are on the edge, my dear! No chance this will work!" Thomas Alden

What are the qualities of leadership?

Curiosity, honesty, confidence, spirit, courage, intelligence, creativity, and vision—these are the qualities that will not only help in leadership, but in life. If your daughter is never known as a leader, she will still need these qualities cultivated for a successful life in whatever field she enters.

When you go back to our movie, you may remember that Amy was precocious and unique. She had traveled the world as a child with her performer Mother. She was exceptional in her perceptiveness, very alert, articulate and wise. She was strong and not easily moved from what she thought, and was able to execute the plan with little to no outside resources. Amy was a leading lady even as a thirteen-year-old girl. She came back into her Father's life in the nick of time because she needed that direction and she needed clarity, but she was engineered as a leader from birth.

There is a stigma placed on decisive, young women, on those who overachieve. When your daughter wants to succeed at something during her lifetime, would you stand in her way and say, "No, that's not done by women?" Or would you champion her cause? The Father who is healthy knows who his daughter is; he knows her limitations and potential. He will recognize uncommon aptitude in his daughter and give her the final pieces for a complete picture of success. The world says, "Oh, she's bossy; you need to do something with her. You need to stop her; you need to shut her down." And Dad says, "No, she's not bossy; she's a leader. Her voice is going to travel, her voice is important, her opinion matters."

Terminology for girls can be bad and limiting. If you see a guy who's strong and boisterous, he's automatically going to be a leader. It's already assumed; because he's strong and vocal, he's going to be an important man someday.

But if a girl is strong and boisterous, she's going to be a wild, non-submissive woman. She's going to be a no-good wife. Her husband is going to get tired of all her talking. I've heard husbands say, "You know, you better get somewhere and learn how to be quiet." And, "You know, you talk too much for a girl."

Don't believe this, Dad, for a moment. Your smart, inquisitive little girl has dominion and leadership built inside of her. Let nothing steal her voice. Let no one muzzle her, keep her silent, or cast a negative light on her because she has an opinion, or a solution, or poses concern about an imminent problem. When you listen and count what she says as worthy to be heard, you will give her the confidence to go against the odds that will inevitably arise and challenge her along the way. You will also teach others to respect her opinion and value her input.

There will be haters! There will be evil people, and others who are just misguided, who want to create a negative diversion for your daughter's passion. They will try to steal her purpose, her passion. There will be shooters, hunters with loaded weapons of hatred, malice, and prejudice. There will be strong winds and adverse weather from time to time. Sometimes the navigational equipment will go out or fail, and she may have to make an emergency landing to regroup and reexamine her flight plans.

I want to point out some subtle parallels between *Fly Away Home* and my life story. In the movie, there was opposition to the geese from multiple fronts. The game warden who threatened the geese's destiny went with his agency's protocol or "doctrine" on the matter. He was the voice of accepted authority, a warden or steward or keeper of government wildlife mandates, good or bad. Some wildlife measures are for the animals' benefit; some are for humankind's benefit and to the animals' detriment. The wildlife officer was not looking outside his mandates; his actions were taken out of pure hatred for Mr. Alden, and not for the good of the geese. In the movie, we saw greed and selfishness, pride and immaturity as an ill-conceived conception of being in charge.

The church world has always been central to my life from childhood. The church has a history of excluding women from the ministry, but my Father believed ministry leadership was for everybody, even women. It was not a popular stance when I was "hearing my call," and it is not a popular stance today, despite the Bible's assertion that young women will prophesy, and despite prophetic and prolific announcements in the latter day that declare women will be a great component of the Latter Day Revival.

At the time of my declaration of a calling, the "officers" of the church, the old guard, had been in power for years without much of a challenge on the issue of women. In all honesty, they thought their stance was for the "protection of the church" and "theological purity." The measures they went to in order to protect the people from fallacy were amazing, and were only limited by the law as to how far they would go to exclude a woman from public ministry. They really thought, and some still do, that this is for the benefit of the local parish and doctrinal integrity; never mind the damage that has been done to countless women who were (and still are) victimized by their misdirected fervor and fallacy.

Another threat to the geese was bulldozers. In their near-suburban Canadian nesting grounds, they faced bulldozers in the name of commerce, and on the coast of North Carolina they were under threat from bulldozers in the name of commerce. This is called capitalism—the dominant way of doing things, fraught with corruption and greed in many cases. In the movie, the developers destroyed the marsh to bring a project to life in the face of resistance.

I need to tell you now, dear Dad, what it is that I do and who my Dad was. I am a second-generation minister and my Father, the Reverend Henry N. Lewis, broke all rules and unspoken plans of bias when he accepted my acknowledgment of a calling to be in ministry also with him. Understand that even today, many mainstream churches do not accept female ministers, and certainly not women in the top leadership spots.

Let me share with you a "bulldozer moment" that occurred between my Father and the dominants of his day, something that greatly affected my destiny. We were part of a church fellowship that was set up for accountability and fellowship, and the ruling officer was called "the moderator." We held our annual session in our building, a church newly built that year. This is where my Dad—in my presence—said to the men, pastors, moderator, and officials, "I'm going to ordain my daughter." He said this directly to the moderator. They then took my Father behind a door; I didn't know where the door went, perhaps to an office, but they kept my Daddy there all afternoon.

The next day, they put my ordination on the agenda, and a discussion was held right in the sanctuary. The matter was held on the floor as a public discussion—and I was the subject of the discussion! I was an adult at this point; I was a grown woman. I was very active in the district; I was a musician, among other capacities. I remember sitting there saying, "This is not going to go well," to my Mother.

She replied, "It's going be all right and he's going to be all right."

The whole district showed up, including all the pastors and the moderator. The moderator was "orating" what Baptists believe, and he was acting like a "bulldozer," driving the people into resistance. There were probably thirty-five pastors there representing their churches, with about 100 to 150 people present in the room.

So they kept this issue of female preaching on the floor for about an hour, and then they let my Dad speak. I don't really remember everything he said, but I could tell by his face that he was not happy. He wasn't beat up, but he wasn't happy.

When he spoke, he said, "Brethren, I did not tell you that my daughter wants to be a prostitute. I did not tell you my daughter wants to do alcohol. I did not tell you that my daughter wants to do something illegal. I said my daughter has been called to preach the gospel. And what you have said is, because she is my daughter, that if I ordain her, you will not fellowship with me."

He just put it out there. "Well, I just want to ask one question." My Daddy was such a good, slow talker, and a deliberate, dramatic speaker.

"I just want to ask you, brothers, one question: What are you going to do when *your* daughter is called to do something that *you* think is just for men? All of you men have daughters. What are you going to do?"

He continued, "But if you choose not to fellowship with me, if you choose not to keep me or don't allow me to continue being part of Calvary, I'm not going to stop my daughter from obeying God."

My Mother stood up and started clapping. She was sitting beside me; I had just left the organ when others began to stand and clap as well. My Father had stopped a bulldozer from overtaking his daughter's mission, at the risk of losing the fellowship he cherished.

Fathers challenge infrastructures. If infrastructures need to be challenged, Fathers will do that. If they see a superficial standard is holding back their daughters, nurturing Fathers take on the challenge.

Let's look at a subtle, third group that also represented a threat to the geese. That group consisted of people who lived in the neighborhood who felt they had no choice but to sell out to the private interests rather than lose everything, thereby eliminating the safe territory for the geese to migrate to for the winter.

"As a farmer, I don't have the luxury of an outside income," one man said at a civic meeting called to discuss the incursion and the development's prospects. "My land is part of the package because I can't make a living off it. If I don't sell, how will I send my children to college?"

This type of resistance did not deter Amy, nor did the resistance I faced stop me.

The pastors, officers, and moderator represented some of the forces in opposition to my destiny in ministry. Doctrine stood against me. Prevailing wisdom stood against me. Most of the laypeople stood against me, either because they subscribed to the patriarchal, doctrinal stance, or because they felt it was in their best interest to side with the powers-that-be.

I have learned that fear is a basic emotion for many people. Fear is the enemy of dreams and purpose, and when people are afraid, they make decisions that are not in the best interest of the greater community's good, but for their own good and protection. They don't always have to agree with the decision, but because there is such a risk in being different, they choose the path of least resistance. Dad, this is why your daughter needs you to understand her purpose and to nurture it, and, if necessary, to risk all to secure her path and passion.

The scenario my Dad and I faced was played out over and over and over. I can remember us going to another fellowship. Daddy had joined with another fellowship, and he started taking me to pastoral fellowship meetings with him. I remember one particular meeting very clearly. It was "for men only," down in the basement. The air smelled like chicken because they were having lunch.

Daddy said, "Come on, you're going in this meeting with me."

Well, the men didn't like it. "This is no meeting for women," one of the men said.

Daddy replied, "Brother Pastors, Brother Moderator, this is my daughter, and she is an ordained minister now. I just want you men to understand and remember that the Baptist Church is autonomous. In other words, we're not governed by denominational bylaws and discipline. Every pastor can pick who's going to be the assisting pastor. This is not governed denominationally, and my daughter is being installed as my assistant pastor. Anybody have any questions?"

He sat down and waited for the combustion. Nobody said another word.

I saw this same resistance too many other times. When it came to my calling, my purpose, my life's assignment, Dad was willing to take on the infrastructure until he died.

I don't remember much else about what my Father was willing to fight against. My Father was advocating for me in a hostile environment, giving me a foundation. It didn't matter to him that in my mind, I wasn't his assistant pastor, because in *his* mind, I was. Never in a million years did I think I would pastor that church. The odds against that ever happening were too great. Today, I pastor the same church my Daddy started. But back then, there was no way in the world I thought that's what I was going to do.

But Daddy knew.

I was his "son," the one who would carry on the church legacy—my legacy.

I still feel like his "son." I had a pastor ask me one time, "Your Daddy didn't have a boy or a son to give it to?"

I replied, "No, I am his son. I'm just in a skirt."

I've been taught not to run from a fight or a challenge no matter how the odds are stacked against me. That's what my Dad did for me. I can go back in my mind and hear all the things my Father would say to me, and how he defined them. When preachers came against me, he went to them and shamed them:

"I haven't said to you men that my daughter is going to be a harlot or that she is going to be a prostitute; I said she is going to preach the Gospel. She's going to preach the Gospel of Jesus Christ. She said that God has called her and she said she's going to preach the Gospel. She's not going to make alcohol or sell drugs. She's going to preach the Gospel. But you want me to silence her because of her gender. "

The "old boys club" mentality is a patriarchal, prejudiced, sexist mindset. In today's culture, a girl is OK as long as she's on her back or in the back of the office, the back of the line or even the back of the church. In that case, she can make all the noise in the world. But don't let her stand up behind the desk of leadership and authority with real power and have men be subject to her. Yes, I know there are many high-profile women in positions of leadership. But the "old boys club" mindset still prevails in corporate America, in boardrooms, in government, in the arts and entertainment industry, and just about everywhere else where we see a plethora of male-dominated roles in finance and business, not just in religion.

If my Dad had allowed men to molest me by robbing me of my vision, or to violate me by setting me down and daring me to speak; or to mentally devour me and disrupt my course, I don't know where I would be today or what I'd be doing.

The first time I stood in that sanctuary, it was so clear again what Daddy had done for me.

The night Dad stood up for me before the moderator, he was quiet when he came home. He was kind of reticent. It was a couple of days before he started talking about what had happened in that meeting, and only after my Mom started asking questions. My Daddy, the Reverend Lewis, was the test case, bless his heart. But he never complained, and he never once asked me to get out of my plane and come down for a landing. He never once asked me to renegotiate my flight plans and settle for less.

When those pastors and leaders no longer fellowshipped with us anymore, I know it hurt him. The men who did not applaud him and who did not honor what he was trying to do had told him they weren't going to come into the church and sit with us as long as there was a woman in the pulpit. They weren't going to do it. And they didn't.

So my Father became almost a solo bird. He never was famous or part of a group. And it didn't matter. He wasn't an A-type personality, but he was a strong man, and he meant what he said and said what he meant. He was willing to stand, even if he had to stand by himself. I don't think he knew that things would be so tumultuous. I think this became clear to him at the same pace it did to me.

My Dad was just working according to his moral consciousness: this is what you do for a daughter. He was in a Father role. He wasn't trying to be a protestant or a revolutionary; he was just being my Father. He'd been my Dad all that time. He didn't take on a fight against a religion or against religious leaders; he took on a fight for his child— for his daughter.

Had I been autistic, handicapped or blind, he would have done the same thing. Had I wanted to be in sports, arts, or even entertainment, he would have stood with me regardless. It just so happened that this was a more divine assignment and destiny, and he was committed to seeing me fulfill it as safely as possible and to seeing me arrive on time at my point of destination.

I don't think Daddies can pick their fights in this situation. Dad, you can't say to your daughter, "Well, if you had been a scientist, I'd fight for you. But because you're a preacher, I don't know what to do with that." You can't abandon her; you can't abandon her no matter what the fight is. Because you're not fighting *against* something, you're fighting *for* her.

My Dad pushed through despite the opposition, knowing what people were saying. He was being my Father. He could have backed down. But that wasn't his calling, or his vision, or his vision for me. He could have turned around and said, "This is going to cause trouble. Maybe we should rethink this."

That's what so many men do. That's what so many men are saying to their daughters. That's what so many men in my day said as well. My Father and I witnessed other situations just like ours, except that when the other men of the church stood against ordaining females, the Fathers told their own daughters, "This is going to cause trouble; we've already seen what it did for Lewis [my dad]. You can do what you want to do, but you just can't preach." Or, "You just can't preach in the pulpit."

Dad was advocating for my calling even before I knew I had one. He championed me to the day he died.

Your Father is the one who gives you the definition of who you are. My Father saw that I was exceptional from my earliest days. He nurtured this in me from Day 1. He nurtured me when I was a child, when I was a ballplayer, and later in my adulthood, when I received my calling. He could see that I was driven and that was uncommon among my peers. My Dad taught *me* to fly, and to provide. When he made me responsible for my siblings, he was teaching responsibility. When he introduced me to adults when I was still a child, he was teaching initiative.

I was always strong. I was always bright and inquisitive. I asked a lot of questions and I did a lot of talking. I remember that someone in the church said to me, "You need to be quiet." My Dad said to her, "Don't tell her that. Let's hear what she has to say." That's how my Dad would protect me from the onslaught of negativity, because I was always a strong girl.

Remember, Dad, you must always be there, not only to monitor your daughter, but more to help her define and interpret situations against all odds.

Recently, some pastors, a couple, reached out to me, so I paid them a visit. I walked into their building and realized I'd been there before. Something had changed; the sanctuary was much larger then, but now it didn't seem so large.

Then I remembered clearly. I "saw" them taking my Dad out of that same room thirty-five years earlier. "Something's changed," I said to the pastor.

"Yes, we moved the door."

It was the door my Father had walked through with the other church leaders. I had not been in that building since that meeting. I asked the current pastor if this building had been built in 1979, the year I had been there previously. It was. 1979 was the year they had told me I could not preach. It was the year that they said no woman would ever preach in their churches, and that no woman would ever preach in *this* church.

It was so ironic that God would have me back here. The pastor said, "You will preach here. You're going to help me with this church. I need your help." I couldn't believe that I was finding myself once again in that same sanctuary.

This was the same place where my Dad had said, "Whatever it costs me, you're not going to hurt my child. You're not going to hurt my daughter." He wouldn't have let them hurt his son, and he made the decision to stand just as firm for his daughter.

It's funny how my life has come full circle, 31 nations later, after multiple opportunities across denominational lines and flying at high altitudes without marring my integrity or my original flight plans.

Dads, when the odds are against your daughter's destiny, don't deviate from the original flight plan for her life. If the "navigational equipment" you thought you could count on goes out, keep letting her pilot her own plane while you guide her by your experience. Her odyssey may be unprecedented and uncharted by the majority, and it might just cost you some exclusion at the risk of her greatness, *but it will pay off.* Dad, don't let the resistance, the loud voices of the majority, steal her purpose or her passion. Create a diversion!

There may be unorthodox signals and strategies required, but do all you can and use all you have to get your daughter flying high and in formation, right along with her male counterparts.

Never give her an option to give up on her dream or destiny.

If she is a leader, teach her to lead; teach her to lead well, and make room in the sky for her at all times, at any cost, and against all odds!

TAKEAWAYS

- What opposition or obstacles is your daughter facing?
- What can you do to help her overcome these obstacles?
- What else can you do to help secure your daughter's future?

CHAPTER 13

● ● ●

They're Really Following Me Now, Dad.

The geese break out of their fence and fly the coop when they see Amy fly away in her new plane. The geese are in perfect formation.
"I don't believe it," Amy says. "It works!"

When a Father stands with a daughter against all odds, it creates a fan base, because people want to see how her life is going to turn out. That's what happens. If a Father believes in his daughter, he'll make everybody else believe in her too – even if they are just following to see what the heck happens.

In the movie, people were excited about the girl and the geese. But it wasn't just the girl and the geese that were important; it was the faith that Amy's Father had in her in the first place that got the whole thing started. Then some bizarre incidents, such as landing on a secured airstrip as a suspected enemy agent and flying through downtown Baltimore on a weekday, spread the word of Amy's amazing journey.

In the end, fans were converging on the anticipated landing site, and television and radio stations were reporting on the event. So there was a lot of buzz about the flight, all because Amy's Father had set her up to succeed. He stood with her throughout her monumental endeavor without thought of his reputation or his own personal greatness. He remained behind the scenes of his daughter's big moment, but her success brought him an affirmation far greater than what he ever could have anticipated.

Dad, when your daughter makes an outstanding contribution and you as her Father prepared her well, her success will get much louder applause than had one of your sons accomplished the same thing. Sons are expected to do well. Sons are accepted and promoted from within the ranks. Men support men better, and they applaud one another's achievements with the hoorays and hurrahs of a sports team.

Success is a male sport!

It's expected that a group of guys will play together as a team to win a tournament. That's the way the game is played. But can a girl get on that team? Can a girl be seen throwing from a pitcher's mound or grabbing a ball for a dunk shot? Can you imagine seeing a girl on a field as the quarterback? Or as a running back scoring a touchdown? No, this is *not* expected. So when your daughter is seen as equal to her male peers, or she is seen carving out her own niche and standing shoulder-to-shoulder in a male environment, it is a greater win than normal. There's a louder sound in the celebration rooting for your daughter, the one you did not abandon or throw away. This is not only her moment but yours too, Dad.

What makes the moment even sweeter is seeing the plan she had coming to fruition, with others engaged and participating in the plan because they see the leadership in your daughter and believe in her. They want to be like her and are willing to be part of her winning team without jealousy or envy, and with sincere adoration and respect. They choose to fly in formation with her. What a moment! The odyssey that began with a few people taking a short journey together now becomes a voyage of thousands, all of whom want to fly with your daughter and get her assistance for fulfilling their own dreams.

Dad, you cannot gauge exactly how much success will come to your daughter when you first begin teaching her to fly. In the beginning of our movie, the goal was getting the geese to a warm place for winter. This goal was simple and pure, and it was easy enough, right? However, it became a monumental task that involved a lot of people, yet brought so many issues to rest.

Protecting a flock of geese brought many people together and catapulted Amy to rock-star status. Learning to fly wasn't the movie's happy conclusion. Learning to fly just got Amy ready for her 1,000-mile journey, which was fraught with peril and destined for an exciting climax. Getting her beloved brood to safety came *after* she learned to fly. The journey, not the learning, was Amy's triumph. It never would have happened had her Dad not been nurturing from the start. He helped provide for the geese, he provided his daughter's wings, and he taught her to use them. On the journey, he stayed with her as far as he could. On the way to the warmth of North Carolina and the safety of the flock, the audience swelled. Crowds of people were running to see Amy land. They wanted to meet her and watch her succeed.

If a Father believes and invests in his daughter, she will acquire a following. Others will want to be a part of the growth and the team when she makes the journey safe and sound, emotionally and physically.

My Father never pastored more than fifty people. He began to do it in his old age along with my Mother, and he did the best he knew how to do to get it started. My parents made a huge investment of their resources and time, but they only had minimal success. They were not well known in any field, and they didn't have the backing others began with—just meager beginnings with a big dream and big faith.

My Dad didn't know that anything would turn out as it did when he began to teach me how to pitch a baseball, or when he began to teach me about economics, or when he took me with him to night school. My parents never travelled internationally, and they never stood in large stadiums or conferences to lecture or teach; they just kept making things happen on the scale of their ability and were quite happy to do so. However, I have done all of these things and more, with thousands now following me from around the world.

What began as a tryst between old systems and present truth turned into a movement that is still in motion today. When my Father was moving in and out of controversy, nobody could have imagined the nations, schools, and acceptance on a global scale that women in ministry and leadership enjoy today.

My Dad's plan for success involved just a small business and the satisfaction of helping a few people. There was absolutely no way he could have foreseen the fullness of this day, and with his little girl at the helm. The Reverend Henry L. Lewis, my Dad, fought long and hard for the equality of women in the ministry, and wherever he saw segregation of gender and bias, he was a loud spokesperson, crying out against its illegitimacy and the victimization of women. He was a Father to six: three daughters and three sons, and he equipped all of them for success. However, his fierce passion was for getting his girls to be strong, viable and unafraid to walk behind the iron door and break the glass ceilings in religion or any other field they desired.

My Dad was a part of the legendary black players of the Negro League. After pitching in the early years with the Atlanta Black Crackers, and then becoming the manager in 1943, he then moved on to the Knoxville Black Smokies in 1945. As an officer, he was fully aware of the pain caused by prejudice and bias. Growing up as an orphan with only an older brother by his side, he prevailed against all odds and became a successful business owner, salesman, husband and Father, and, in later years, a statesman of the Church.

I remember hearing his painful yet heartwarming stories of being a southpaw in a league where right-handed pitchers were better paid. Yes, he had to overcome some internal issues of abandonment, rejection, instability and failure, and he also had transitions in relationships. But he prevailed over the odds and excelled at becoming a great human being and a phenomenal Dad.

Being a great Dad doesn't always begin with a great life. You can still become great after many mistakes, trials and errors of manhood, but you cannot hide your flaws from your children. You must tell them what it took for you to become unstoppable, and then give them the same skills so that they can move toward their own destinies, despite any weaknesses and missteps along the way.

What did it take for my Dad to become as solid as a wall? What obstacles did he overcome to prevail and save his children from the plight of fear and anonymity? I don't know everything about this, but I do know that it wasn't easy. He never knew his own Father and Mother. He never knew any aunts, uncles, or cousins. Nor did he ever meet his paternal or maternal grandparents. And he was unsuccessful in personal relationships until he mastered his feelings of low self-esteem and self-worth.

Dad never finished high school until he was an older man. But while poverty and no education would seem to be guaranteed combination for failure, my Dad was unstoppable. Once he was sure of his footing, he communicated his skillsets to me and to the rest of his children. His desire was to see all of us unhindered by distractions, delays and disappointments. He wanted to see us free from mental anguish and emotional stress, walking in love, focus and favor.

What a legacy!

Dad, you too can overcome any and all failures and be the model Father your daughter needs you to be. It's not your mistakes that keep you from being what she needs; it's how you view your mistakes. The way you see yourself after making an error gives you either optimism or pessimism. Overcoming your mistakes is key to being the Dad you were always meant to be. Not allowing the DNA of failure to reside in you is a powerful decision that you must make. Your daughters especially need you to be the hero for their plights, and you can do that in a big way when you overcome the fear of failing again.

When your daughter is able to fully embrace her calling and destiny, many people will be waiting on her to do so. You cannot imagine what will happen when she finally lifts off and begins to soar with confidence; motivate her to move forward with the fire in her bosom to make her mark. She's confident, yet tender; passionate yet balanced; focused and intentional; yet she has the swagger of a woman who knows how many people are awaiting her arrival.

In my first few months at the helm as CEO of the small business, we saw exponential growth. My Dad lived a good long life to see some of the successes, and of course he always told people that he had made the right decision "putting that girl in place."

I remember one particular Sunday when my parents were still alive. Suddenly, there were no more parking spaces. The streets were lined on both sides with cars and the inside of the sanctuary was swarming with people. During the buzz of preparation for the service, we were all looking for my

Mother. Suddenly, a scream came from the front of the building outside, and I recognized the bone piercing, high-pitched shrill as my Mother's voice.

Dad was with me and we looked at each other, stunned and wondering what in the world was wrong. I ran toward Mom's voice and found her outside the building, tears flying off her face. I was startled and looking around for any possible danger that could get her so upset.

"Mom, what is wrong?" I asked.

"Wrong?" she replied. "Nothing is wrong. I am counting the cars and I cannot keep count. Where are all of these people coming from? How did they find us? Cars are everywhere! Oh, my goodness! I never knew that we would see this day!"

People were literally swarming and flocking to our door. My Dad, having come outside to survey the situation, started greeting people, shaking hands and reveling in the success of the moment.

People have continued to come to this day. How did this happen?

It happened because my Dad stood by me and never allowed anybody to deter me. He didn't allow anyone to molest me, physically or spiritually. I know he had a great reward in heaven.

The business continues to grow today. I have travelled and spoken to crowds of as many as 100,000 people, in twenty-nine nations. I have stood on the stages of success with some great people, and I have been able to see some great exploits in my day. I have launched so many people— both men and women—into their careers and destinies, and I continue to do so, breaking barriers and going places where women were previously rejected or denied admission.

The gender barriers still exist. There are those who believe their life's work is to reestablish the walls of segregation and gender bias, yet I still prevail. I look around and see hundreds of women coming on strong in my field of leadership and at my level of authority within the Church at large.

A few months back, a prominent man of the cloth asked me, "Why are you so different? You are not angry, or full of revenge or malice. What makes you so balanced and seemingly unruffled? You are patient and kind, yet very powerful. What's the difference between you and some of the other women in different fields of leadership?"

I pondered my answer, and then replied, "My Dad taught me to fly, and I recognized more and more the gratitude in my heart for the fact that he did that."

"Well, I will do likewise," he said, "I have three daughters myself, and just watching you tells me I need to do the same for them that your Father did for you."

Like Father, like daughter. Dad, it works!

Teach your daughters to fly, and you will never regret it!

TAKEAWAYS

- Is your daughter reaching the moment when you can release her to fly on her own? How will you celebrate that time with her?
- What do you envision your daughter's flight path to look like?
- How can you help ensure her success?

CHAPTER 14

● ● ●

Mom's Imprint

"You're strong, just like your Mother!"

In *Fly Away Home*, Amy's Mother took care of her for the first twelve years of her life. Amy went around the world with her Mother; she was provided for and educated; she was fearless and articulate; and she was an independent thinker. She was happy; she wasn't in a balled-up position over her circumstances and she wasn't maligned. Mother had done a good job because Amy was OK. In fact, although it was her Father who built Amy her plane, her Mother had imprinted her all along and prepared her for life. Even though Thomas Alden had walked away from his responsibility, Mom had done a good job with this child.

Her Father didn't have to teach her how to conquer fear; he didn't have to teach her how to speak up. Even Amy's nurturing skills were in place, as you learn in the movie when she discovers and nurtures those geese. Amy's Mom had done a great job.

As a child, I was in an ideal situation; I had both Dad and a phenomenal Mother. My Mom was the epitome of a Proverbs 31 woman: her value was above rubies and she could do everything well. She loved the children, loved her own life, loved my Dad, and loved others that she touched and nurtured. "Mrs. Lewis," as my Dad lovingly referred to her, was a queen and a lady. She was never afraid, that I knew of, and she was smart, kind and really special: articulate and fancy, with skills in almost every area. She could sew, cook, keep a beautiful home clean, decorate, design, farm, can, make summer and fall wines, and pray the sweetest prayers ever. My siblings and I were truly blessed, and we had Mother with us on the earth until all of us were grown and on our own.

She was a tremendous voice in our home and in our neighborhood. She owned and operated her own beauty salon and did all the women's hair in our community. She was an advocate for orphaned children, invalids, and the poor. A tremendous role model and imprinter, she also supported my Father in all of his endeavors. She gave me her sincerity and strength, her zeal for life, and her appreciation of cosmetics and perfumes. She also taught me the ways of business and entrepreneurship, along with how to cook a slamming peach cobbler with homemade ice cream.

In a perfect world, a Mom and a Dad nurture the children together. But when the order is reversed, and Father isn't present, Mommy can still do a great job. Women can raise healthy, happy girls.

In the opening scene of *Fly Away Home*, Amy appears happy and satisfied to be with her Mother without her Father's presence. It is indeed possible for a girl to be healthy, whole and happy when her Mother is the primary caregiver.

While the Father should be the leader of the home, when he refuses to fill that role, a balanced Mother can raise a healthy daughter who succeeds. If the Dad does walk away and the circumstances are such that the Mother is the primary imprinter, she can still raise a great daughter. Someone must teach her to fly, even without a Father.

So Mom, if you find yourself in the position that you must raise your daughter, you can do it, and do it well.

My Dad was there, and he was leader and provider and all those other good things. My Mother, meanwhile, was a tremendous nurturer of us all. She was also very perceptive. She saw my bent early. My bent, my proclivity, was gifting, and my Mother really nurtured me emotionally by validating and affirming me and giving me the space to talk, to ask questions. She was very smart, and she always had good answers. I could sit all day talking to my Mom, just asking questions.

Now, my Father set the boundaries. My Dad gave me the guidelines. But my Mother always gave me good answers. I was very precocious as a child, so I was always "all over" everything. I was smart and I had a lot of questions, a lot of inquiries. My Mother was a beautician, and I always wanted to learn to do hair, so I became a shampoo girl in her shop. I wanted to learn how to cook, how to wash dishes; I wanted to do everything my Mother did. A Mother can play a huge role in teaching her daughter to fly.

Mom, let me give you some tools you can use for helping your child to soar, which will make you very proud.

First, you have to make sure that you meet the basic needs a Father-provider was intended to fulfill. You have to provide, and you have to discipline. Nurturing your daughter as a single Mother means you have to be both good guy and bad guy. Boundaries, guidelines, punishments and permissions are now *your* job. And as a Father would, you must also be proactive in maintaining the relationship. When your daughter sulks, you need to take action. Don't wait for your daughter to come to you; make the initial steps toward keeping your relationship healthy. That means you MUST talk and you must also listen. Communication is critical for a single Mom and her daughter. It's also a challenge, so *how* you communicate also matters. Here are some simple tips:

1. Be an active listener. Active listening involves reflecting back what someone else is saying instead of assuming you already know that person's viewpoint. Also listen "to the feelings underlying the message," and don't be hasty. Your daughter may be talkative, and if she is, let her "get it all out."

2. Agree to disagree. Moms and daughters disagree on many topics, such as dating, marriage, parenting and careers, and each usually tries to convince the other to change opinions. Believe me, there are some subjects you will never agree on, but don't be angry at one another. Learn not to be defensive or abusive, and be sure to listen and really care about what you are hearing.

A daughter doesn't have to change her mind all the time to please her Mom; and Mom doesn't have to change her opinions, either. Work through it together.

3. Stick to the present. Don't bring up old, hurtful moments again and again. When you are sharing with you daughter, stick to the issue at hand; don't bring up old mistakes, old broken promises, or anything else that can make communication hard.

4. Don't be accusatory. Include yourself in the examples. You might say, "I feel this way," or, "This is how that makes me feel." Similarly, avoid sarcasm and be careful not to exhibit a lack of seriousness at an improper time. Such attitudes are easily misinterpreted, cause hurt feelings, and take you further away from resolution.

5. Show your love. Remember to praise your child. Give her unconditional love and support. Set aside time each day to play, read, or simply sit with your child.

6. Create a routine. Structure—such as regularly scheduled meals and bedtimes—helps your child know what to expect.

7. Set limits. Explain house rules and expectations to your child—such as speaking respectfully—and enforce them. Work with other caregivers in your child's life to provide consistent discipline. Consider reevaluating certain limits, such as your child's permitted amount of screen time, when she shows the ability to accept more responsibility.

8. Don't feel guilty. Don't blame yourself or spoil your child to try to make up for being a single parent.

9. Take care of yourself. Include physical activity in your daily routine, eat a healthy diet, and get plenty of sleep. Arrange time to do activities you enjoy alone or with close friends.

10. Lean on others. Work out a carpool schedule with other parents. Join a support group for single parents or seek social services. Call on trusted loved ones, friends, and neighbors for help. Faith communities can be helpful resources, too.

11. Stay positive. It's OK to be honest with your child if you're having a difficult time, but remind him or her that things will get better. Try to keep your sense of humor when dealing with everyday challenges.

12. ALWAYS send positive messages about the other sex. Don't bash men when talking to your daughter. Give her an optimistic view of men and teach her to relate to them in positive, proactive ways. If her Father is alive and willing to be in her life, always encourage his presence and celebrate each moment he spends with her.

13. Look for opportunities to be positive. Point out the accomplishments or positive characteristics of members of the opposite sex in your family, in the community or even in the media. Avoid making broad, negative statements about the opposite sex.

14. Contradict negative stereotypes about the opposite sex. Share examples of members of the opposite sex who don't fit those stereotypes.

15. Include in your life members of the opposite sex who aren't romantic partners. Seek out positive relationships with responsible members of the opposite sex who might serve as role models for your child. Show your child that it's possible to have long-term, positive relationships with members of the opposite sex.

Being a single parent can be a challenging but rewarding experience, and with patience and support from others, your imprint will help your child to thrive.

Moms are strong. Remember that you conceived and birthed the baby, and that it took strength to do that. You are strong and you can give your daughter your strength. Mothers can validate their daughters. Mothers can still train them. Mothers can teach them to cook, to make them independent. Moms can do that.

Remember that in the movie, before her Mother died in a tragic car crash, Amy was a balanced child. She wasn't crazy. She was happy, smart, cultured and articulate. Single Moms can raise balanced children. They can give their daughters wings. You, Mom, can have a phenomenal relationship with your daughter.

Show her how to give, how to serve, how to find the joy in servant-hood, and how to help others. Make her big on the inside.

As her primary imprinter and caregiver, find creative outlets for your daughter's talents. When I was growing up, I was a young pianist. My Mom purchased an upright piano for me and took me to music lessons when I was four. When I didn't have the words to say things, my music helped me communicate, and it served me well as a talent all through high school. One of the best things you can do for your daughter is to encourage her growth: academically, artistically, emotionally, and spiritually, so that she will be well rounded in many areas. Don't stifle her because it's something you may not be good at. Find a mentor or coach for things you are not comfortable doing with her. She will need a ground team all of her life, so don't try to be everything to her. Connect her socially to other people and venues, so that in the end, your daughter is a self-reliant, strong female.

Now, Mom, if you are single and you want to date: PLEASE BE CAREFUL! I cannot stress this enough. Teach your daughter through modeling how to treat and be treated by the opposite sex. Discretion is vital. Never have a man stay with you overnight in your daughter's presence. Don't date multiple partners at the same time. Remember that you are imprinting her: as a female, as a woman, as a wife, and as a Mother. Be wise and discreet in all of your personal affairs. Don't make your daughter your best friend, the one with whom you share everything. Don't be chummy now; be her imprinter and role model, her "she-ro." As she gets older and begins to fly, you will have plenty of time for that other type of relationship with her.

I honored my Mother's word when I was young, and I still do now. She was so wise and smart, and I always wanted to use her methods. Her ways were for the good of all and whatever she did seemed to work out at home, at school, and at church. She was brilliant. Have your daughter value your voice. As her role model and nurturer, give thought to the advice you render to her. Make sure you always do your due diligence when advising. You want your words to have favor and your child to harken to your voice and model your ways. Be a modest woman in your dress, speech, and behavior. Be a culture advocate, exposing your daughter to the finer things in life: the arts, the stage, music, museums, comedy, drama, fine arts and more. Don't hold back from introducing her to a brand new world through the cultural climate of your city. Introduce her to ballet, sports, jazz, and opera, to name just a few. Your daughter can be a well-adjusted, well-loved and well-cared-for child without her male parent present.

I did not want to close this book and not speak about the very important role of the Mother, the other woman in this scenario. I cannot omit Mommy's role, because it is so vital for a daughter to have a female imprint on her life. This is the finishing touch that brings the class and the inner-core strength to your little pilot for the rest of her life.

Dad, avoid tension with the Mother of your child. And Mom, don't compete for Dad's attention with your daughter. That can yield negative emotions and a lack of forgiveness for years between Mom and daughter that is many times passed on to the next generation, making the girls in the family weak and sick with bitterness and unnecessary grief. The ultimate goal is a godly outcome for the entire family.

I do realize that not all family models are ideal or close to perfect. Moms can miss it; Mom can be a nightmare if she suffers from her own Father-hunger, abandonment issues, or rejection. If Mom is an addict, manipulative, or compulsive, it can wreak havoc on all involved. But if there is any good, any praise, or anything positive in the family mix, highlight it and strengthen it for the good of all.

The child comes through the Mother, and the child hears everything in vitro. The baby hears. In the womb, your daughter is very aware of nurturing and love; she is very aware of her Mother's desire for her—your love for her. Science proves that in vitro, the child is listening. So the medical field encourages Mothers to speak to the child, laugh with the child, and sing to the child, all to strengthen the child.

I've birthed two beautiful daughters, and they're both very strong. I remember them both when they were in the womb, and I sang to them, played music, spoke to them daily and prayed over them. Imprinting begins in the womb, Mom. My daughters are phenomenal women: smart, sassy, and successful. I didn't always have their Dad with us, and at vital times in their lives their Father was missing-in-action. But I knew they would still be great, so I sacrificed and raised them to be healthy, and I am so very proud of both of them. They have their wings and they fly high in so many arenas.

In the movie, when Dad Alden is on the ground, ready to release his daughter to go without him, she hesitates and asks him, "Can I really do this?" He replies: "Yes, you absolutely can, Amy; you are like your Mother: strong, fearless, and smart. I know you can do it, because I see all of her in you."

Everyone recognizes powerful imprinting from a powerful Mother: both those on the ground and those in the sky! Mommies NEVER take their hands off of their children.

Dad builds the aircraft but Mom, YOU are the wind beneath her wings!

TAKEAWAYS

- Are you, consciously or unconsciously, projecting negative attitudes or unfavorable stereotypes about the opposite sex in your actions, general demeanor, or when you talk to your daughter?
- What can you do to revise those unfavorable stereotypes or attitudes?

Chapter Endnotes

[1] Franklin B. Krohn and Zoe Bogan, "The Effects Absent Fathers Have on Female Development and College Attendance," *College Student Journal* 35, no. 4 (December 2001): 598-.

[2] E.M. Krampe and P.D. Fairweather. "Father Presence and Family Formation: Atheoretical Reformulation." *Journal of Family Issues* 14.4 (December 1993): 572-591.

[3] Christine Winquist Nord, DeeAnn Brimhall and Jerry West, *Fathers' Involvement in Their Children's Schools*, NCES 98-091, U.S. Department of Education, National Center for Education Statistics. Washington, DC: 1997.

[4] U.S. Bureau of Labor Statistics National Longitudinal Survey Program, "America's young adults at 27: Labor market activity, education, and household composition: Results from a longitudinal survey," news release, March 26, 2014.

[5] Brady E. Hamilton, Joyce A. Martin and Stephanie J. Ventura, "Births: Preliminary Data for 2012," *National Vital Statistics Report* 62, no. 3 (September 6, 2013): 3.

[6] Arlene F. Saluter, *Martial Status and Living Arrangements: March 1995*, U.S. Census Bureau: A-15.

[7] Statistical Abstract of the United States, 1996, 1997, U.S. Bureau of the Census.

[8] Ibid.

[9] Ibid.

[10] "Child Abandonment," Thompson Reuters FindLaw, http://criminal.findlaw.com/criminal-charges/child-abandonment.html (accessed September 3, 2014).

[11] Doug Dante, "Analysis of Friend of the Court Custody Recommendations," http://www.scribd.com/doc/6169001/Analysis-of-Friend-of-the-Court-Custody-Recommendations (accessed September 3, 2014).

[12] Rick I. Johnson, *That's My Teenage Son: How Moms Can Influence Boys to Become Good Men* (Revell, 2011).

[13] Stephen Stosny, "Anger, Men and Love," *Psychology Today,* April 5, 2010. http://www.psychologytoday.com/blog/anger-in-the-age-entitlement/201004/anger-men-and-love (accessed September 4, 2014).

[14] Ibid.

[15] Ibid.

[16] See note 12.

[17] Joseph Mattera, "Traumatic Traits of Fatherless Men," http://josephmattera.org/traumatic-traits-of-fatherless-men/ (accessed September 4, 2014).

[18] Ibid.

[19] Ibid.

[20] Ibid.

[21] Dr. O'Shan D. Gadsden, "How Growing Up Fatherless Can Impact Current Relationships," The Good Men Project, http://goodmenproject.com/guyhood/how-growing-up-fatherless-can-impact-current-relationships/ (accessed Sept. 4, 2014).

[22] Mark Banschick, "The Narcissistic Father: How a Narcissistic Dad Can Affect Your Life," *Psychology Today*, March 13, 2013. http://www.psychologytoday.com/blog/the-intelligent-divorce/201303/the-narcissistic-father (accessed September 4, 2014).

[23] Ibid.

[24] Matt Moody, "What Is Selfishness? What Is Narcissism? Are Human Beings Selfish by Nature or by Nurture?" Changing Your Stripes, http://www.calldrmatt.com/AskDrMatt-1203.htm (accessed September 4, 2014).

[25] Diana E. H. Russell, *The Secret Trauma: Incest in the Lives of Girls and Women* (New York: Basic Books, 1986), 231.

[26] Anne Paulk, *Restoring Sexual Identity: Hope for Women Who Struggle with Same-Sex Attraction* (Eugene, Oregon: Harvest House Publishers: 2003), Appendix B.

[27] See note 1.

[28] *Getting Men Involved: The Newsletter of the Bay Area Male Involvement Network,* Bay Area Male Involvement Network, Spring 1997.

[29] "The Consequences of Fatherlessness," National Center for Fathering, http://www.fathers.com/statistics-and-research/the-consequences-of-fatherlessness/ (accessed September 5, 2014.)

[30] U.S. Census Bureau, *Children's Living Arrangements and Characteristics*, March 2011, Table C8, Washington D.C.: 2011.

[31] "Information on Poverty and Income Statistics" (brief), Department of Health and Human Services, September 12, 2012.

[32] *Survey on Child Health,* U.S. Department of Health and Human Services. National Center for Health Statistics. Washington, DC, 1993.

[33] John P. Hoffman, "The Community Context of Family Structure and Adolescent Drug Use," *Journal of Marriage and Family* 64 (May 2002): 314-330.

[34] Warren R. Stanton, Tian P.S. Oci and Phil A. Silva, "Sociodemographic Characteristics of Adolescent Smokers," *The International Journal of Addiction* 7 (1994): 913-925.

[35] Stephen Demuth and Susan L. Brown, "Family Structure, Family Processes, and Adolescent Delinquency: The Significance of Parental Absence Versus Parental Gender," *Journal of Research in Crime and Delinquency* 41, No. 1 (February 2004).

[36] Sandra L. Hofferth, "Residential Father Family Type and Child Well-Being: Investment Versus Selection," *Demography* 43, no. 1 (February 2006): 53-78.

[37] Gunilla Ringbäck Weitoft and others, "Mortality, Severe Morbidity, and Injury in Children Living with Single Parents In Sweden: A Population-Based Study," *The Lancet* 361, no. 9363 (January 2003): 289-295.

[38] Jean Beth Eshtain, "Family Matters: The Plight of America's Children," *The Christian Century* (July 1993): 14-21.

[39] C. Osborne and S. McLanahan, "Partnership Instability and Child Well-Being, *Journal of Marriage and Family* 69, 1065-1083.

[40] K. H. Tillman, "Family Structure Pathways and Academic Disadvantage among Adolescents in Stepfamilies," *Sociological Inquiry* 77: 383-424.

[41] Christine Winquist Nord and Jerry West, *Fathers' and Mothers' Involvement in Their Children's Schools by Family Type and Resident Status. (2001). Washington, D.C.: U.S. Department of Education, National Center for Education Statistics.*

[42] Edward Kruk, "Father Absence, Father Deficit, Father Hunger: The Vital Importance of Paternal Presence in Children's Lives," *Psychology Today* (May 23, 2012). http://www.psychologytoday.com/blog/co-parenting-after-divorce/201205/father-absence-father-deficit-father-hunger (accessed September 5, 2014).

[43] C.S. Hendricks and others; "The Influence of Father Absence on the Self-Esteem and Self-Reported Sexual Activity of Rural Southern Adolescents," *ABNF Journal* 16, 124-131.

[44] Karen Heimer, "Gender, Interaction, and Delinquency: Testing a Theory of Differetial Social Control," *Social Psychology Quarterly* 59 (1996): 39-61.

[45] Heather A. Turner, "The Effect of Lifetime Victimization on the Mental Health of Children and Adolescents," *Social Science & Medicine* 62, no. 1, (January 2006): 13-27.

[46] C. Knoester and D.A. Hayne, "Community Context, Social integration into family, and youth violence," *Journal of Marriage and Family* 67 (2006): 767-780.

[47] *Journal of Family and Economic Issues* 14 (Summer 1993): 163-186.

[48] See note 1.

[49] R. Lohr and others, "Clinical Observations on Interferences of Early Father Absence in Achievement of Femininity." *Clinical Social Work Journal* 17, no. 3: 351-365.

[50] See note 1.

[51] See note 43.

[52] Jay D. Teachman, "The Childhood Living Arrangements of Children and the Characteristics of Their Marriages," *Journal of Family Issues* 25 (January 2004): 86-111.

[53] See note 1.

[54] See note 1.

[55] See note 42.

[56] Claudette Wassil-Grimm, "Where's Daddy?: How Divorced, Single, and Widowed Women Can Provide What's Missing When Dad's Missing (Overlook Press, 1995).

[57] Paul L. Adams, Judith R. Milner and Nancy Ann Schrempf, *Fatherless Children* (New York: Wiley & Sons, 1984).

[58] See note 1.

[59] J. Elium and D. Elium, *Raising a Daughter* (Berkeley, California, 1994).

[60] See note 1.

[61] See note 1.

[62] See note 1.

[63] See note 1.

[64] See note 1.

[65] See note 1.

[66] See note 1.

[67] See note 1.

[68] See note 56.

[69] Henry B. Biller, *Fathers and Families: Paternal Factors in Child Development* (Praeger, 1993).

[70] *BLS Reports*, U.S. Bureau of Labor Statistics (2013): 2

[71] Glenn Llopis, "4 Skills That Give Women a Sustainable Advantage over Men," Forbes.com, http://www.forbes.com/sites/glennllopis/2011/08/22/4-skills-that-give-women-a-sustainable-advantage-over-men/ (accessed September 6, 2014).

[72] Jack Zenger and Joseph Folkman, "Are Women Better Leaders Than Men?" *Harvard Business Review* (March 2012), http://blogs.hbr.org/2012/03/a-study-in-leadership-women-do/ (accessed Sept. 7, 2014).

[73] Population Reference Bureau, "Analysis of Data from the U.S. Census Bureau," *2002 through 2012 American Community Survey*.

[74] Ibid.

[75] Ibid.

[76] "Digest of Education Statistics," Table 3-10, National Center for Education Statistics, http://nces.ed.gov/programs/digest/d12/tables/dt12_310.asp (accessed September 7, 2014).

[77] "Women CEOs of the Fortune 1000," Catalyst (August 27, 2014), http://www.catalyst.org/knowledge/women-ceos-fortune-1000 (accessed September 7, 2014).

[78] Kate Zernike, "She Just Might Be President Someday," *New York Times* (May 18, 2008).

[79] "Meg Whitman Profile," *Forbes*, http://www.forbes.com/profile/meg-whitman/ (accessed September 7, 2014).

[80] Scott Allen, "Mary Kay Ash – Most Outstanding Woman in Business in the 20th Century," About.com, http://entrepreneurs.about.com/od/famousentrepreneurs/p/marykayash.htm (accessed September 7, 2014).

[81] The Mary Kay Car Program, PinkLighthouse.com, http://www.pinklighthouse.com/2008/04/the-mary-kay-car-program-2/, (accessed September 7, 2014).

[82] "Estee Lauder: The Sweet Smell of Success," *Biography*, documentary film.

[83] "Oprah Winfrey," Wikipedia.org, http://simple.wikipedia.org/wiki/Oprah_Winfrey (accessed Sept. 10 2014).

[84] Susan Harrow. *The Ultimate Guide to Getting Booked on Oprah* (Harrow Publications, 2004).

[85] Susie Mackenzie, "Woman of Mass Derision," *The Guardian* (March 10, 2006).

[86] Bill O'Reilly, *The Radio Factor with Bill O'Reilly*, Westwood One (October 17, 2006).